LESSONS:
THE WISDOM WITHIN EACH MOMENT

LESSONS:
THE WISDOM WITHIN EACH MOMENT

By

Teresa Sue McAdams

R. C. Linnell Publishing

Lessons: The Wisdom Within Each Moment

© Copyright 2012 by Teresa Sue McAdams and Licensors

All rights reserved. No part of this book may be reproduced or used for any reason or by anyone without permission. The only exception being small excerpts from the book that will be used to glorify and promote it.

Cover design by Dave Davis

ISBN 10: 09840025-3-7
ISBN-13: 978-0-9840025-3-5

Published by
R. C. Linnell Publishing
Louisville, KY 40205
www.LinnellPublishing.com

Other publications by Teresa Sue McAdams:
Co-author of Today's Journey Tarot www.todaysjourneytarot.com

Contact her:
https://www.facebook.com/teresa.s.mcadams
Teresasuemcadams@gmail.com

For my wise and beautiful daughter, Joy
and my partner in all things, my husband, Ben

Introduction

Every moment we are alive is an opportunity to take advantage of a lesson being offered. We either can or we can't, we either do, or we don't – and it doesn't matter. The lesson will be presented again and again and each time it is we may learn something from it – or not.

Many people consider life as a series of tests that we pass or fail. They acquire guilt and lack of confidence for the ones they fail and that builds up over a lifetime until even the smallest of challenges seem monumental. Their ego feeds on those lessons passed and yet there is very little satisfaction or happiness associated with the success.

I see life as a series of lessons for which there are no tests.

In 1989, I was asked to contribute an article to a newsletter. I wasn't given a topic or theme. It happened to be my daughter's eighth birthday so I wrote about some of the things I was learning from her. I titled it "Lessons." From that experience I realized how significant the moments in our lives are and the multitude of opportunities there are for learning in each of those moments. I continued to write the articles for various publications.

These little stories are some of my lessons over the years. I was encouraged to gather them together and although they were not written that way, I have placed them in chronological order of when they happened or how they occurred to me. The stories are as historically accurate as my memories of them allow. But that doesn't matter either. What matters are the lessons that I learned, or didn't learn, or am still learning from each moment of my life.

SECTION ONE

I wouldn't have it any other way.

Starting when I was about three years old, I spent a lot of time fishing with my grandparents. They loved to fish and owned a small lake outside of town. I can still see them sitting on their little red folding chairs. I can smell Granddad's pipe and the scent of Grandma's cologne. They bought me my own cane pole with a little red and white bobber that floated not far from the shore. I felt so happy and safe with them and I always managed to "catch" the biggest fish. But I usually wasn't sitting like they were. Oh, no. I was stomping around their chairs and eyeing every bug or poking a stick down a crawdad hole. Grandma would say that I must be quiet if I expected to catch a fish, but I paid little attention. There was just too much to see and do! Eventually Granddad would have enough and rather sternly repeat Grandma's request. Granddad was my buddy, and so rarely did he discipline me that I paid attention when he scolded. I sat down on the ground and stared at the bobber. Sure enough, it began to move. I squealed and Granddad shushed me. Eventually, with his help I pulled in the biggest catfish caught to date in that lake. What a big deal they made over me! They bragged about it for weeks. I guess we have to be quiet and watchful in order to manifest our "prize catch." If we aren't paying attention or making too much noise (if only in our busy minds) it can slip right on by.

It seems to me, there are a lot of things we have to do in life that we just don't want to. I've often wondered why it is so. Wouldn't it be wonderful to just go through life doing only what we want and having everything turn out okay? Rainy Saturday mornings always remind me of walking to my piano lessons when I was a little girl. It was about a three-block journey and as I remember it, it was always raining. I sloshed through the puddles dreading the inevitability of arriving on the massive front porch of my teacher's home. She was never really mean to me. But she was very, very old and her house smelled very, very funny. The only things in her living room were a gigantic organ and a piano. She played for all the funerals in town and sometimes as I approached, I could hear the mournful strains of the organ a block away as she practiced. I wasn't very good at practicing at home so there was always this moment of disappointment and strict discipline that rained down on me like the weather outside. I begged my mother to let me quit going but from the time I was six until I was twelve, and my teacher finally retired, it was my weekly lot to withstand the ordeal. I wasn't very good at the piano and I just could not understand why I had to do what I truly dreaded.

Years later when my daughter, Joy was eight years old she begged for piano lessons. I began to research the teachers in our area and her grandfather bought her a used piano. As the piano was delivered, I told her that now we'd have to make some calls and decide which teacher she would like. She just paused and looked at me and said, "Mama, I want you to teach me." Introducing my daughter to the joy of making music is something that I very much wanted to do. Eventually we got her a "real" teacher but for a while it was just she and I and the piano. Gosh I'm glad for rainy Saturday mornings.

Some children have a tough time on their first day of school. They cry and cling to their parents. I was not one of those crying children. My mother walked me to school and I couldn't wait to let go of her hand and run into my classroom. I should have been one of those crying children. I was shy and timid. But I think I was so excited by what might lie behind those red brick walls that it never occurred to me to be upset. It was all that I expected. I can still remember the smell of that first classroom – the huge blackboard and crisp new books. I remember my teacher's sweet smile as she greeted each one of us with a pat on the back. I also remember another little girl huddled in a corner crying. I couldn't imagine what in the world she was crying about! There is a quote that means a lot to me. "It is our resistance to what is that causes us pain." I think it may be our "perception" of what is that causes us pain. Whatever we expect is exactly what we get. When we change our perception, everything in our world changes.

My father was proud to say that he had never taken a vacation or day off from work. That was true the whole time I was growing up. We never went on vacation and, besides going to church on Sunday, rarely did anything as a family. So, the one summer he took us to see fireworks on the Fourth of July really stands out in my memory. I was probably six or seven. My father worked for his parents and I'm sure that was a complicated arrangement that I'm still sorting out. The only time he was off work was when their store was closed – which wasn't often. But they did close on the Fourth, along with everybody else in those days. For some reason, my father loaded my sisters and me into the car just before dusk and drove to the county fair grounds. We parked out in a grassy field along with everyone else in town and he even let us climb onto the hood of the car –

something that usually would have been taboo. I remember the feel of the cool glass as I lay back against the windshield and saw my first real fireworks display. But it is not the fireworks that I remember today. I couldn't even tell you what they looked like or what the car looked like. I only remember that once on the Fourth of July he took me to see fireworks.

Our expectations are built up so high around the holidays that it is impossible for them to be fulfilled. Suppose we did get just what we wanted for Christmas?

Barbie looks pretty good for her age. She didn't have townhouses or swimming pools when she first came on the market. The most expensive accessory was a case to put her clothes in and the wedding dress at $5.00 was a coveted item. One Christmas when I was about eight, Ken was born or evolved or whatever fashion dolls do. I asked for a Barbie and a Ken for Christmas. I went to my mother. She said I could have either a Barbie or a Ken doll but not both. Well, I had to have Barbie first. I mean, what could I do with Ken without Barbie? And I wanted Ken. I had to have both – it was the only way. I begged Mother unmercifully. She held firm that we could only afford one doll. I worried. What would my friends think if I ended up with only a Ken doll? I'd not be able to show my face. I finally told Mother I didn't want any dolls for Christmas. Nevertheless, I watched under the Christmas tree. Mother was always so slow at getting the presents out. Finally one day two Barbie and Ken size boxes appeared. Did I dare hope? I couldn't be sure. I worried. The day finally came and, sure enough, Mother had given in. Both dolls were there. It didn't feel as good as I thought it would. I had Barbie and Ken, but Mother couldn't afford any doll clothes. She promised to try to get someone to make some homemade clothes. Ugh! That was even worse. I watched my friends dress and undress their dolls in all their fancy clothes – which is all Barbies are good for anyway. All my dolls had were the clothes on their backs. (Swim suits back then.) I got exactly what I wanted. Barbie and Ken lived out their days in the back of my closet.

When I was a little girl there were two major rules that had to be followed. One was that I could not cross either highway that bordered our neighborhood. Because my grandparents owned a grocery just a few blocks from my school, the other rule was that I could not shop at a rival grocery store. There was another small grocery close to the school too – on the other side of the highway. All of the cool kids went there after school. I was told that they had the biggest selection of candy ever – even though the place wasn't much bigger than a hole in the wall. You know what happened. One day the temptation was just too big. Clutching my quarter, I followed the other kids and waited at the edge of the highway. I was scared. I'd never crossed before. Finally, the traffic cleared and I ran for it. I heard the screech of tires and looked into the windshield of my uncle's car! He was white as a sheet. I quickly moved on, hoping he had not recognized me. It didn't even occur to me how close I'd come to being hit. With my head full of "what ifs," I pulled open the screen door of the grocery and looked in. What a dump! Even at ten years old, I knew I didn't want to buy anything there. It was dirty and smelly. I backed away and guiltily headed toward home. As I rounded the corner of my block, I saw my uncle's big black car in our driveway.

You know, if you feel that something isn't right, the Universe will give you every opportunity not to pursue it. If you do it anyway – knowing it isn't right – you will manifest your own punishment. And that's the only punishment there is. My uncle was so shook up and my parents so upset that I could have been hit by a car that I was not punished - other than a stern "do not do that again." I never did.

Growing up in my family's grocery store meant that my sisters, cousins and I all worked there at one time or another. The store closed when I was eleven so I was always too young to work the cash register or other important jobs. My father taught me to stand on a chair behind the counter and bag groceries – brown paper sacks back then. It wasn't as easy as it sounds. He had strict rules for just how the groceries were to be bagged and I knew better than to do otherwise. First, the heavy things, like canned goods always went in the bottom of the bag. They made up the foundation of the bag; what everything else rested on. Some of those cans were very heavy. People seemed to lug a lot around with them.

Another rule was that anything leaky or runny, like some meats (although as the butcher, he wrapped stuff pretty tight) and frozen items that might thaw a little were to be wrapped in brown paper before being put in the bag – to keep other items clean, I guess. All cold or frozen things had to be put together in one bag. Cold things keep other cold things cold, he said. It didn't really matter how many bags you had, it was distribution that was important. Everything had to be balanced so the bags wouldn't rip and the customer could carry them easily. Soft stuff like bread and fruit went on top so it wouldn't get smashed by the hard stuff and stuck out of the top of the bag like it was the most important item there. If the customer had kids along, stick a free sucker or penny candy in the bag to make a good impression. Oh, and volunteer to carry the bags to the car – every time – no matter how strong the customer may look. I hauled a lot of groceries. So let's see: the hard stuff is the foundation but needs to stay on the bottom. The soft stuff is more precious and needs to be protected from getting smashed by the hard stuff. Messy things need to be wrapped up tight so they don't leak onto other things. Cold attracts cold. Balance is the most important thing. Give away for free and always offer to help. I think that about covers it. Maybe my job was important after all.

On Valentine's Day all the kids would bring boxes to elementary school that they had decorated (with help from Mom and Dad) to receive Valentines from their classmates. Schools may still do that today but there were a couple of huge differences. In my day, the students' boxes were judged by the teachers and the "best" box was awarded a prize. Also, the kids themselves picked who to give or not give Valentines to instead of bringing one for everyone in the class. I dreaded the day. My parents were never inclined to help me decorate a box so I always opted for a shoe box covered in tissue paper with a few odd construction paper hearts pasted on. I was always embarrassed to exhibit my box next to the architectural wonders brought by certain kids. You know the ones. And then there was the pressure of the Valentines themselves. What if no one gave me a Valentine? Should I pass my cheap Valentines out to just the kids I considered safe or go for it and give them to the ones I'd like to like me? All the boxes were lined up on a table in the back of the room (this happened every year – no matter what grade I was in) and after the cookies and Kool-Aid, we were free to open our boxes and survey the cards inside. I always got some Valentines from the kids that were basically the same status as me (not at the bottom of the caste system, but no where near the top). There was never anything special that said I was special to anyone. Every year the same scenario played out and every year I trudged home on that day and tossed my few treasures away feeling very unloved. I wish I'd known then that all the love I need is already inside of me. I wish I'd known then that the Universe itself is comprised solely of love and no one has to give it to me. I wish I'd known then that although people would love me, no one needs to give me love because I already have it. It is already mine. It sure would have made Valentine's Day a different kind of day for me. It would have been a day to celebrate myself.

The house I grew up in had a crooked front walk. It was sort of an "S" curve from the porch steps to the street. I've often wondered how that came about. My great uncles built the house around 1939. Maybe they just wanted to do something different for their nephew's house. Maybe at the time my dad liked the idea. By the time I arrived, fifteen years later, my dad loathed that sidewalk. It was different from all the other sidewalks on the block and made his house stand out. That was something he didn't like one bit. He often talked about taking it out and putting in a straight sidewalk. But for most of his life his money went to more important things – like raising three daughters. So, for all of my childhood I heard about the walk. After my sisters and I grew up and things were better for him financially he finally did have the walk changed and the house had a perfectly straight sidewalk like every other house in the neighborhood. I loved the old walk. It was perfect for racing model cars or building little towns that had a "valley" in between. The curves were fun to maneuver on the stilts that my dad built or you could jump the curves altogether if you were good enough on roller skates. So much of my childhood took place right there on that front walk. Everybody's sidewalk (path) through life is different. Some people strive for years to conform and that's okay – it is their choice after all. Me, I think I would have left the sidewalk exactly the way it was.

There was a woman who lived next door to my parents when I was growing up. She was the personification of the "wicked witch" of the neighborhood. All of the kids feared her and knew not to step one foot on her property or she'd come after us yelling and waving whatever implement she happened to be working with. Sometimes when I was playing in my own back yard, I could feel her watching me. She and my father had many disputes over property lines or trees shedding on her lawn. Once when Dad put a swing up in a tree that bordered her front yard, you would have thought he'd broken the law from the fuss she made. She often came over and screeched at him about one thing or another that we kids had done. He would just mumble and curse under his breath and go on about his business. I knew he didn't like this woman. The grownups never discussed the situation in earshot of us kids, of course. I only caught the essence of his impatience with her. I just wished she didn't live there. Years later, after I'd grown up, I was surprised when Dad mentioned that she had remarried. Remarried? I didn't know she'd ever been married. Dad explained to me then that she had married her high school sweetheart shortly before he left for WWII. He didn't come home. She'd been a widow for many years. Wow. I pondered that for a few days and everything began to make sense. How unhappy and lonely she must have been. How she must have seen all the kids in the neighborhood as the children she'd never have. I'm not excusing her behavior. Sometimes it helps to have compassion when you know why a person acts the way they do. Since finding out about her life, I have tried to be more compassionate when people act in an ugly way. When the waitress gruffly takes my order, or a clerk in a store rebuffs me, I just shrug it off thinking that perhaps they have a reason I will never know for acting like they do. I know I was sorry that I never acted kinder toward my neighbor when I was a kid. Because really, the reason people act the way they do isn't important. It is only important that I act with kindness since I just don't know what is going on in their lives. After all those years Dad became friends with his neighbor and her new husband. All past squabbles were forgotten. They all remained friends the rest of their lives.

We never went back to school until after Labor Day. Kids go back a lot earlier now. By mid summer, parents are already buzzing the stores to find supplies and new school clothes. It has become a very big deal and a boon for retailers. There wasn't much preparation then either. A few days before school started we went to the local variety store and bought whatever books were required. We only got new supplies when our old ones wore out so I used the same pencil case and notebook for more than one year. My mother usually ordered one new outfit from the Sears catalog – for the first day of school. That was about it. We were scooted off to school with very little fanfare. I never liked school much after the first grade. I think now that it was because I became disillusioned rather quickly. Many of my teachers were – shall we say – less than adequate.

The standards expected of teachers now were not quite in place back then. So, unfortunately, I didn't always do my best. I've never been good at doing what didn't make sense to me or obeying rules for the sake of rules. I've never been able to respect authority that didn't deserve respect. And most of all, I've never been able to "fit in" or play along to get along. If it didn't make sense to me I just didn't do it. No one ever told me that seeing something differently could be an attribute so I was in trouble a lot. Everyone tried to make me conform. It was hard then. But now I wouldn't have it any other way.

One of the things we had when I was growing up that we don't have now is time. Everyone is very busy these days and it is hard to find time to just relax and do nothing. In my childhood it seemed that we didn't have to plan for time off, it just happened because of the way the world was. Summer has always been hot. But before there was central air in every home, it was especially hot. My mother did everything she could to keep our house cool. She had thick thermal curtains that she pulled over the windows each morning to keep out the sun and the heat. Of course that also blocked the air – if there was any. We had window fans (until the sun beat through the window and the curtains were yanked closed) and she never used the oven or cooked too much to bring more heat into the house. By evening though, the temperature inside the house was very uncomfortable. We escaped outside until dark. Everyone had chairs in their front yards then. My parents occupied our two and my sisters and I usually sat on the porch steps or I played around in the yard. Mother often brought the newspaper out with her but Dad just sat and watched the world go by. Everybody in the neighborhood was sitting out too. Sometimes people would stop by but usually everyone was in their own yards, just sitting and talking and doing nothing. I love air conditioning. I'm not advocating a return to those sweltering times. I guess we'll just have to figure out our own times to do nothing.

When I was a little girl one of my best friends was a big, old, weeping willow tree that stood in our back yard. I played under it for hours. Its long sweeping fronds made an ideal fort or castle. Its gnarled trunk was a mountain I could climb. I would lose myself for hours beneath its fronds and lie supported and safe on its strong, knotty limbs. Most of my future dreams took shape there and many of them were acted out in play. The other kids in the neighborhood played beneath the great tree too, but no one else seemed to share our special bond of love. When I was about seven my father announced that he was cutting the tree down. I was devastated and loudly voiced my objection. He claimed that the tree had bugs and there was nothing else to do. The bugs would kill it eventually. The limbs would rot and it would be dangerous, especially to the kids who always played around it. I believed he wanted it down because it stole water from his garden. He had often complained "that danged old tree" was taking all of the ground's moisture and the garden was wilting. I suspected it had more to do with his gardening ability than my tree. I begged and pleaded and appealed to my father through my tears that he find some other way. Couldn't we kill the bugs? He shrugged off my despair and the tree came down. I didn't believe him that the tree was dying. But I knew I was. I stayed in my room until it was over and every last limb had been hauled away. No one understood, especially my father. For forty-five years I have grieved the loss of this tree and blamed my father for a selfish act. Then recently I remembered something. The year after the tree was gone my father suggested that we plant a flower garden in the remnants of its trunk. He helped me and indulged me as I picked just the right flowers and just the right pattern to honor my absent friend. We planted that garden every year until I lost interest as I grew into a teenager. I wonder how much of what we believe is selective memory? The pain of most situations is a strong force that overshadows everything else as it takes up residence in our subconscious. I truly forgot that my father tried to turn a negative situation into a positive for me. Or maybe it was there all along. Maybe my love for my father endured because the part of me that was not angry remembered.

I used to dread going back to school every year. Now, I realize all kids hate going back to school. But I really hated it. We always started back near or on my birthday. That was bad enough, but on top of that, I also had to go through the name thing. My parents did a cruel thing to me. They called me by my middle name. Until I started school, I wasn't aware that I had another name besides Sue. No one ever explained it to me. Teachers were adamant to call me Teresa unless I corrected them. If I didn't correct them, they would continue to call me by the name that had no meaning to me. I was painfully shy and it frightened me so much to put my hand up on the first day of school and ask a stranger to change what was written in ink in her book. Some years it took me days to work up the courage. It never got better. Every year, I'd have to repeat the same routine. I felt I'd been cursed. When I got to college, I decided I couldn't face it anymore. I'd let them call me Teresa or whatever else they wanted, just so I didn't have to go through the pain of correcting them. When I sat down in that first class and the professor called the roll, was I ever in for a surprise! "Miss McAdams?" he called. Who? I thought. In that instant I realized how foolish it had been to hold on to my name and continually correct people, insisting that I was Sue. Since then, I've married, taken my ex-husband's last name, divorced and gone back to my maiden name and chose to keep my maiden name although I've married again. Many people don't understand that.

But I've grown accustomed to my name. They gave it to me, I earned it and finally I'm comfortable with all three parts. It's okay if I'm called Mrs. Whatever, too. See it just doesn't matter. My name is not me. It has nothing to do with who I am so it doesn't matter what it is. It's merely a tool of identification. I wish I were going back to school this fall.

My father loved to tell the story about how he learned to swim. It is a bit cliché. His older brother and some of his friends literally threw my father into a lake when he was about eight or nine years old. I guess my father had been scared of the water up to this point. It was definitely a case of sink or swim. This was in the early 1920s. We'd never think to do this to a child today. Older brothers being what they are, it may still happen from time to time. My father chose to swim and became a very good swimmer – an activity he enjoyed most of his life. I'm not advocating this technique for learning anything, of course. But I do think it demonstrates that we often underestimate what we can accomplish or what would be available to us if we just "took the plunge" and overcame our fears. I believe any of us can do anything. The only thing that ever holds us back is fear. If something takes away our fear or we choose to ignore it, just think what we could accomplish!

I distinctly remember the day the church burned. I think I was about nine or ten. We had been to church that Sunday morning as we did every Sunday. My mother was in the kitchen fixing dinner. I was in my room when I heard her let out a yell. We only lived four houses from the church and she could see the roof and steeple from the kitchen window. She was one of the first to see the smoke. We rushed down the street and watched with the gathering crowd as flames engulfed the building. The volunteer fire department did their best and for a while we thought something of the pretty little church might be saved. But I remember the anguish as we watched the final assault. The steeple fell with a crash into the sanctuary. When I was not in school or at home, I was at that church. My mother was Sunday school superintendent and Dad was a deacon. We went to Sunday services and Sunday school of course, choir practices, youth groups, Bible school, Wednesday prayer meetings. Almost all of my friends were members there. Almost all of our activities centered in that building. I was taught that our church was the "right" one. Other people were misguided in some way and our way was the only way. I worried about that. I worried about all of the people who didn't go to our church. What was to become of them? After the fire, other churches in our town readily stepped forward and offered their facilities for our activities. It felt very weird going into places that were not only forbidden to me before but were considered less that "right." It took about a year to rebuild, so we moved from church to church while the construction was going on. I was amazed at the generosity of the other congregations. I was confused that all the other churches looked pretty much like ours on the inside. Some were nicer. Some were plainer. All had hymnals and pews and classrooms and everything else exactly like we had. I could see no difference. So many lessons came out of that experience that I couldn't begin to list them. Most importantly, I began to think for myself for the first time. I realized that all people were just like me even if they believed differently. I probably didn't comprehend the changes occurring within me. I was just happy that when we moved back to our church, the old wooden pews were gone and replaced with nice new padded ones!

I spent every Thanksgiving of my childhood watching the parade on television. Mother would park the rest of us in front of the TV to keep us out of her way in the kitchen – not that I didn't enjoy the parade. It was an adventure from start to finish. You never knew what was coming next – clowns, balloons, fabulous floats, marching bands, or famous stars. People were packed along the streets – filling the sidewalks with joyous abandon. Sometimes there would be long delays as the entries ran to catch up and fill a gap in the flow. Sometimes people made mistakes – balloons would escape, floats didn't quite hold together, bands would be off the beat. It was all wonderful. Throughout the whole thing I knew, at the very end, there just might be a visit from Santa – the real Santa. When that magical moment arrived, it was never disappointing. Today, however, we get a much more manufactured version. It is more like a commercial than a parade. Only the best highlights are shown – the Broadway plays and such – and you don't get the feel of the journey down the parade route. I suppose you might if you were actually there watching from the street. Does anybody do that anymore? Does anybody really enjoy the journey as the parade marches by? Or are we only tuned into the glamorized highlights – the best of the best? Mistakes are seen as undesirable and often we miss the delight of the spontaneous results. And the ending! What are we looking forward to – magic? Sometimes I think not. In my childhood, watching that parade, I never doubted that Santa would be there at the end and he always was.

SECTION TWO

There would always be more to life than I could ever imagine.

Christmas wasn't always special in my house growing up. With money tight and both of my parents being rather "high strung," the holiday season was generally a disappointment. I remember one year… I was around ten years old and so longed to be "big" like my older sisters. The one closest to me had just turned sixteen and what a wonder she was to me. I tried to tag along with her and her friends, but was usually rebuffed with the delicacy only a teenage girl could express. She did such cool things and went to so many cool places. For Christmas that year, I begged for my own pair of ice skates. Skating was one of my sister's favorite things. I thought that if I had my own skates, maybe she'd take me along. I waited anxiously for Christmas morning. I had no indication from my parents that the ice skates might be there but by some miracle, there they were under the tree. It just so happened that year was especially cold and a light snow had fallen on Christmas Eve. My sister saw my skates and got the wonderful idea that we'd go that very day to the town lake and skate. My parents were outraged that she would want to leave on Christmas but somehow she talked them into it. I know now that she just wanted to get out of the house, but that day I thought she was doing it just for me. She called her friend, who already had a driver's license, to pick us up and we headed for the lake. Many neighborhood kids were already there and the snow had been pushed back to make a perfect circle in the center of the lake. My sister snapped at me to hurry and lace my skates and left me sitting by the side of the frozen lake. I had no idea how to lace those skates. I sadly watched as she and her friend headed for the center of the lake without me. But then, she turned and glanced back my way. She said something to her friend and they both came back to the bank. They hurriedly laced my shiny new skates; each took one of my hands and they dragged me out on the ice. We skated for a long time that way and I quickly gained my balance. Then my sister showed me how to touch my toe down just so and stop. She let go of my hand then and I hesitantly skated by myself across the lake while my sister followed close behind. Before we left that day, while I was unlacing my skates near the car, I looked up and saw my sister, spinning and gliding across the lake. Her long dark hair was flying out behind her from underneath her earmuffs and the pink pompoms on her skates bounced happily as she skated towards me. I realized that I had just experienced one of the best Christmases ever and while I loved my new skates, they were not the best gift I had received.

When I was eleven, my grandfather died. I have vivid memories of this time that turned my world upside down. It wasn't a bad death. He died in his sleep after fishing all day – something he truly loved to do. He owned a grocery store where I spent as much time as I did in my own home. When he died, my parents decided to close the business since the age of supermarkets was upon us and the store was already struggling to compete. My father eventually got another job at a factory and all turned out well, but I missed my grandfather and his store. I didn't like the changes that had been thrust upon me. I remember him well. He always smelled like the pipe he smoked and he wore scratchy wool cardigans that I snuggled up against when I sat with him in his big chair. What I remember most was the story my father often told. My grandfather had worked for many years for a chain of grocery stores and when he was fifty years old, he was fired for being too old to work there. It was the late 1930s and jobs were scarce. He scraped enough money together to start his own modest grocery business. He had a new angle, too – he bought a building several blocks from the town square and featured a large paved parking lot. Stores had always been located on the town square with limited parking. He called it "McAdams Drive-In Market." Over the next thirty years he became very successful. The impact of his life and death and that story has never left me. Every time I think that I am too this or too that to do something new, I remember. Sometimes, I even smell the faint scent of his pipe.

For most of us, change is an enemy that we constantly try to avoid. Even when we make a change voluntarily, like taking a new job or moving, we struggle to adjust and complain about what is different from our old situation. My father was someone who resisted change. He went to work for his father as a young man and although he hated the family business, he stayed for seventeen years. When my grandfather died and the chance arose to get out, Dad actually planned to keep the store open – even though he was terribly unhappy there and we were struggling to make ends meet. It was my mother who put her foot down, raised the roof and just about every other cliché imaginable to make a change happen. I can still hear the shouting! One of my most vivid childhood memories is the struggle she went through to get my father to take another job. I'm not sure what she finally used to convince him – I probably don't want to know – but he finally succumbed. Best decision he ever made, he'd say over and over again for years. He loved his new job and was quite successful. It wasn't the first time Mother stepped in and forced him to change. He loved to tell the story about how after years of dating, she finally threatened to leave him for good unless he married her. He told her he didn't have the money for the license. She loaned it to him and they got married. In 1938, I believe a license was two dollars. All my life he talked about moving. There were so many things about his house he didn't like. But he lived in the same house for fifty five years – until he died. Maybe because of his example I have a sense of what change is really all about. It is not something to fight against, anymore than we can fight sunrise or the first winter snow. Change is the human condition. We are meant to change. We have to in order to grow and learn. It is not the change that causes us pain; it is our struggle against it. I often wonder what my parents' lives would have been like if my father had been willing to make changes and how that would have changed me.

I loved to ride my bike during the summers when I was growing up. I rode it all year long when it was possible. I loved the feeling of freedom as I sailed through the streets of our town. I loved the air moving through me as I moved along. I loved meeting up with my friends and sitting on our bikes at the street corner and just gossiping the afternoon away. I loved to explore the streets I'd never been down or paths that might lead to discovery. My bike was independence from the restrictions of my parents and I reveled in it. From the time I was about six until I was sixteen and bicycling was no longer "cool," that bike was one of my very best friends. Today bikes sell for thousands of dollars. My bike was a conglomeration of parts from old bicycles of my sisters. My father pieced it together and painted it a rather ugly shade of blue. The only embellishment was a banana seat that was all the rage at the time and I had to beg for that. Funny though; it didn't matter a bit that my bicycle wasn't one of the newest models or that it shimmied a bit when I rode it too fast, as I often did. It wasn't the look or style or latest technology that made that bike special. It was how I felt when I was riding it. No amount of money could have bought that.

I remember the Thanksgiving when my grandmother "ruined" the dinner my mother was cooking. The conflicts between them started long before that day. My parents spent the first year of their married life living with my paternal grandparents. My mother didn't know anything about cooking and my grandmother, being thoroughly scandalized, set about to make that right. Mother just wasn't very domestic, but Grandma was a domestic perfectionist. Dad used to say often that you could eat off her floors. (Who'd want to?) I'm not sure what took place during this time, but it created a tension between these two women that lasted the rest of my grandmother's life. My grandparents never came to our house for dinner – ever. My mother, who eventually became a pretty good cook, was never comfortable in the kitchen. We ate simple meals and Thanksgiving was always a stressful time for her. When Grandma was old and alone my parents felt obligated to invite her to our house for Thanksgiving dinner. Mother never allowed anyone else in the kitchen while she was cooking, but Grandma insisted upon hanging around anyway. I was probably twelve years old that year. The one job I was permitted to help with was breaking the bread for the dressing. I can still see Grandma sitting at the table watching my mother's every move.

Mother sat the pan of uncooked dressing on the table while she turned her back to baste the turkey. Grandma grabbed a spoon and took a little taste. She decided it needed more pepper. She gave the container a mighty shake and the lid fell off. A mound of pepper fell into the pan. My mother was furious. Grandma just laughed. I quickly got a spoon and began scraping the pepper off the top of the dressing. Of course, my grandmother didn't intend to ruin the dressing. Or did she? We always do exactly what we intend to do – even if we don't intend it consciously. Whatever is buried in our subconscious finds a way to materialize and express itself – resentments, anger, or even jealousy. Whatever we do is exactly what we intend. Wouldn't it be better to look for the hidden cause and eliminate it than to disown our actions by saying we didn't intend for something to happen? That is the only way we can be assured of having control of our future actions. We are responsible for what we do – even when it is "unintentional." Grandma was banned from the kitchen after that incident. The rest of us ate the dressing and swore it was just fine.

Everyone always complains about winter. The temperatures seem colder than usual and the snows just kept on coming. Sometimes in the middle of a season like that it is hard to believe that spring is just around the corner. There are signs everywhere if we just stay aware. I've mentioned before that my grandparents had a corner grocery store when I was growing up. My dad was the butcher and I spent a lot of time hanging around and "helping" with stocking shelves or whatever else needed to be done. Every year in early spring my father put out a display of kites. Now these were not very special kites. I think they sold for about a nickel and were made of the flimsiest materials. But they were always brightly colored and came collapsed so that you had to put the kite together and make it air worthy. As soon as the display went up, I began begging for a kite. My father would always put me off by saying that it was still too cold and the kite would never fly. I knew in my heart when the kite display appeared it was already spring – no matter what the weather outside was doing. I was relentless in my begging and sooner or later Dad would give in and let me have one of the kites. It's funny, but I don't remember ever actually flying one. I remember taking them home and putting them together and then they sat in my room until my mother finally threw them away. I guess flying the kite wasn't actually the point. The point was recognizing a sign of spring and acknowledging that sign by bringing one of those kites home and making it mine. Then no matter the weather, I had spring in my heart.

When I was around twelve, my job after school was to go to my grandmother's and walk her dog in the field behind her house. I cannot tell you how much I hated that job. There were a million things I would have rather been doing – riding my bike, watching TV – the usual after school activities. The real reason was that the dog, Pedro and I hated each other. I had been so excited when I heard that my uncle had gotten a dog for my grandmother. My parents had never let me have a dog and I couldn't wait to finally get to spend time with one. When I went to Grandma's the first time to meet Pedro, it was a shock and a disappointment. He was a brown Mexican Chihuahua, as fat as he was long with big brown protruding eyes that glared at you. He was an older dog and very set in his ways. The first thing he tried to do was bite me. I was scared of him – with good reason. But here I was, ordered to take this dog to "do his business" every day after school. As I stood in the field day after day while Pedro took his time, circling and circling and "pretending" to have found the right spot, I watched an apartment house being built on the other side of the field. One day after it was finished and people had moved in, I saw something move near the second floor windows. As I watched, two of the most beautiful creatures I had ever seen glided out of the windows and gracefully climbed down an outside staircase. I stared in awe as they moved around to the front of the apartment house and out of my view. Often we forget that even in the worst situations, the Universe always offers us something positive. The alluring creatures were Siamese cats. I have had a Siamese cat in my life ever since I was twenty years old and out on my own. I can not imagine life without one. Before that day in the field, I didn't even know they existed. Perhaps if I had not been there in that field with Pedro, I never would have known what they would mean to my life.

The fact that words can incite strong emotions and even actions has been proven throughout history. We have learned over the last few decades to speak more politically correct and most of us cringe at the words used in the past to describe us and humiliate our fellow human beings. Now that degrading words of race and gender and class may be taboo, our speech has reached a new level of permissiveness. Anything goes on talk shows, "news" reports, even award shows on TV. Our political candidates and business opponents somehow deserve the angry and often untrue things we say and do. I wonder if we realize that every word spoken has an energy of its own. If we think a negative thought about anyone, the energy of that thought is released into the Universe. The Universe does not discriminate nor discern what our intent may be when we utter a curse under our breath at someone. My father was the least violent man I've ever known. He never owned a gun or even went to war. And yet he had two favorite sayings when he didn't like someone or the way someone acted: "They aught to take them out and shoot them" and "He ain't worth killing." He said that about politicians, ethnic groups, people he knew in town and every boy I ever dated. Now, he never would have wished anyone's death intentionally but those phrases he uttered had emotion behind them. Do we ever say, think or act unintentionally? That is a huge question, but I believe we do not. Every energy we expel from ourselves has emotion behind it and therefore intent. Like attracts like, so every energy in the Universe is attracted to each other to form larger energy gestalts. Can these energies eventually become so powerful that they "take on a life of their own" and do harm? Another good question. So I ask myself why. Why is it necessary for us to casually speak harmful words and produce negative energy? Why do we pollute the Universe with our judgments, insecurities and anger? Can we not disagree without rage? How would the world change if just one of us stopped?

Do you remember what it was like the last few weeks of school as you anxiously awaited summer vacation? It was hard to concentrate on school as the weather got warmer and the days got longer. You thought it would never end but eventually the bell rings the last time on the last day. Summer was finally here. Do you remember how the long days and weeks of summer stretched into an endless world of play and discovery? Can you smell the cotton candy at the county fair? Can you see the fire flies as they light up a night in June? Can you feel the prickly grass beneath your bare feet? Do you remember the joyous refreshment of home made ice cream or fresh squeezed lemonade? Can you feel wind flying through your hair as you rode your bike or the coolness of the water in a neighborhood pond? Ah, Summer. How we adored it. How we looked forward to it. And it never let us down. At least, not until we were older and our expectations were greater. At least, not until we were older and our summer days blended into the other seasons as we drudged through our days. At least, not until we were older and we forgot to remember.

In many ways my mother was way ahead of her time. She was very

intelligent, well read and educated. I'm not sure how well that served her because she was a product of her times. Society dictated she acquiesce to a male dominated world and unhappily she did just that. For many years, she was a housewife, ruled by the decisions made by my father. I benefited greatly from her knowledge and foresight although I am only now able to appreciate if fully. One of the things she knew absolutely even as far back as the 1950s was that the Earth was in trouble. She also knew that through education we could change the course of the impending destruction. She started with her own children. One of the worse things we could ever do was to throw trash out of a car window. Everyone did that then. No one thought anything about it, but Mother used to say that someday we'd all be buried in our litter. She always picked trash up wherever she was. Heaven help us if we left a light on in an unoccupied room or let the water gush down the drain while we rinsed dishes or brushed our teeth. She reused everything – bread sacks, jars, wrapping paper, newspapers. Part of that had to do with saving money. She was raised on a farm with nine siblings. But she would always talk about waste, waste, waste. Wasting anything – food, clothes (unfortunately I was the third child), toys, you name it, was completely forbidden. Dad always laughed because he'd know what was going to be in his lunch all week by what Mother fixed for Sunday dinner. When awareness was finally raised about environmental conservation, it was nothing new to me. I'd heard it all before and felt really good about the fact that most of it was already second nature to me. My mother wasn't an easy person to live with at times – for a lot of reasons, and she and I often clashed, but I'm grateful for the lessons she taught me and my little corner of the Earth must be grateful, too!

As the Christmas holidays approach each year, we all begin to think a lot about gifts. We wonder what to give and if we're honest, we wonder what we'll get! As I was going down my list one year, a thought occurred to me. I have so many gifts. I'm not talking about the usual – love, health and happiness, although those are great gifts. I was thinking about all the things I have now that I never would have expected. For example, I grew up in a house without air conditioning. No one had air conditioning in their homes then. We didn't have a dish washer or clothes dryer. We hung clothes out on a line after washing them in a wringer washer. Not only didn't I have a cell phone as a teenager, our house was on a party line. I sometimes had to wait for hours just to use the one phone situated in a communal hallway where everyone could hear. Imagine having my own phone in the palm of my hand! We had two TV stations and to switch between the two we had to go outside and turn a cold antenna pole. No microwave, no TV dinners or convenience foods of any kind, and no personal computer. We had to wait weeks for a letter to be answered instead of messaging at an instant. We only had one car, which my dad drove to work. Everywhere we wanted to go, we walked. I had to wear dresses to school and pantyhose hadn't been invented yet (I may still have indentations in my legs from garters!). I listened to a transistor radio that was bulky and awkward to carry. Now my MP3 player is part of my phone and oh yes, there's a camera in there too. We thought Polaroids were a miracle! One of the best gifts I have now is fast drying nail polish – oh what a joy not to sit around and wait for nails to dry. Many of the things I use every day now would have seemed like a dream to me then. I never would have imagined them…ahh…do you suppose…we sometimes limit the gifts that come to us because we can't imagine them?

I have never been to the Kentucky Derby, even though I have lived my whole life in the Louisville area. It is a big deal around here and a big deal for the horse industry. I've said many times that I'd like to go, but only if I had box seats – which isn't likely since they are so expensive. Many people spend Derby Day in the infield, but while affordable, not my idea of a good time. My attitude about the Derby is probably a "gift" from my mother. She went one time as a young woman in the late 1930s. The whole time I was growing up she would retell the story every Derby. She was in the infield with thousands of other people and only saw the rear end of a horse one time. She said it wasn't worth it. She was very disappointed and declared that going to the Derby was a horrible idea. My mother's experience and her attitude about it have had repercussions for sure. It makes me wonder how many times our experiences are shaped by our expectations. Many people go to the Derby and never see a horse but still have a great time. Mother was there on a beautiful spring day. She was young and healthy and with her friends. But because her expectations weren't fulfilled she didn't consider that there might be other experiences worth having there. Because her expectations weren't fulfilled she was grumpy and sour on the Derby the rest of her life. Because her expectations weren't fulfilled, I've never been to the Derby.

I grew up with two older sisters. They are five and six years older than me. For the most part this wasn't a bad thing. I sometimes felt as if I had three mothers. But, all in all, they paved the way for me and clued me into things my parents would never have told me. There was one thing that bugged me. Whenever I wanted something or tried to do something or behaved in ways that were not to my parents' liking, my father always said, "We didn't let 'the girls' do that, or go there, or get away with that and we're not going to let you either." This frustrated me to no end. It was an argument stopper that had no reply. It meant that when I expressed myself as an individual, I was oftentimes thwarted right from the start. These were everyday things, mind you. If I wanted to stay out a little later or wear a certain type of outfit or push any boundary just a little bit, I was reigned in. If I tried to do anything different from my sisters, I was made to feel as if I was wrong. Unfortunately for my parents, this backfired on them. By the time I was a teenager I was – in their view – quite rebellious. Looking back, I realize I never did anything very shocking (at least not to me) but I did bend the rules quite a bit. You see, I wasn't my sisters. It may have been easier for my parents to judge me by those standards but for me it was unfair and terribly stifling. I just wanted to be me and to be listened to and understood as me – not as an extension of somebody who had gone before. I did the only thing I could. I pushed those boundaries and fought for my individualism. I think anybody would have done the same.

I am now an avowed cat lover, but throughout my childhood my biggest desire was to have a dog. Yes, I begged and pleaded and used every tactic available to me. But my parents would not be moved. They had already had several dogs while my older sisters were growing up. By the time I came along, they didn't feel the need to go through the dog thing again. No matter what I tried, my parents' unwavering attitude was that they weren't doing it again. I understand their point – now. They had a lot going on and really couldn't handle another major pet (I had turtle and goldfish substitutes). When I was fourteen, a friend's cat had kittens. You guessed it. I marched in the house with one and declared that I was keeping it! Charlie had a long life and was still residing with my parents after I moved away. Funny how someone else's decisions shape the people we become. Maybe becoming a cat person instead of a dog person isn't a big deal, but I wonder how many other things about me are shaped by the decisions of others – not only my parents but teachers, friends and even casual acquaintances? What motivates those decisions? Do I accept who I am without wondering who shaped my likes and dislikes, my attitudes and beliefs? If they didn't come from my own experience, they may not belong to me at all.

My mother was always a serious walker. She walked hard and fast. I imagine she developed this skill due to her diminutive size. She was just four foot eleven. If she wanted to keep up with "normal" sized people, like my father who was six foot, she would have to move faster. When she decided to lose weight, I was in middle school. It was natural that her choice of exercise would be walking. She walked everywhere in our small town – to work, to church, to the grocery, to the town square. She power walked years before the term was coined. She always came home frustrated because so many people stopped to offer her a ride. In a town where everybody knew everybody, the good neighbors naturally became distressed seeing Mother trudging along with her bags of groceries or in the rain or whatever. She never accepted the rides of course: it would defeat the purpose. It annoyed her to no end that people wouldn't just let her trudge along on her path. I think our egos are like those good neighbors. As we plod along through life, focused on a spiritual goal, the ego continually stops us with good intentions. Don't we want to ride? The ego may look like a good friend we'd like to spend time with or a warm car on a cold day, or respite when we're tired. It may offer a short cut home or the latest gossip or even an alternative route – a way we've never been before. None of these things are wrong or bad. If we are focused on a particular goal, perhaps we should learn how to use our will to choose to keep walking. There are other times for the ego to take us for a ride.

Some people believe fairy tales are based on fact. I learned very young that it is true. I also learned that fairy tale endings depend on being in the right place at the right time. Let me explain. When I was very young and roaming the neighborhood looking for something to do, an elderly neighbor lady invited me into her home for tea. My parents weren't particularly neighborly people so they didn't know this woman other than to nod a hello. It wouldn't have mattered if they did. I was not allowed to go into anyone's home and not allowed to eat at anyone else's house. Never one for following rules, I sheepishly ventured into her kitchen. It was a wondrous place. The house was spotlessly clean and smelled like a combination of mothballs and cookies. I had never had tea and I felt so grown up drinking from the little china cup. The tea was delightfully sweetened with honey and a plate full of freshly baked cookies instantly appeared in front of me. She was as sweet as the tea. I remember how gentle and kind she was as she listened to me babble on about things that are important to an eight year old. I went to her house several more times although I never told my parents or anyone about it. Then I suppose I lost interest in tea and moved on to other things and soon my afternoon teas were forgotten.

When I was fourteen, I was invited to the prom by a very special boy. My father absolutely forbid me to go – as I had expected. I made all the usual arguments and then stopped speaking to him altogether. I'm sure if he could he would tell you that I eventually wore him down. He finally gave his permission just a few days before the prom. I was devastated. I had no dress and I had no money. Dad, in his wisdom, suggested I wear a bridesmaid's dress my sister had only worn once. Just imagine for a second what a bridesmaid's dress looked like in 1968! It didn't fit and it had this bow thing in the front…but what could I do? Mother didn't sew and a seamstress would be too expensive. It was hopeless. Then, from somewhere, a memory of something popped into my head. I suggested to my mother that our neighbor (was she still alive? I asked first) sewed. I remembered seeing her machine and many works in progress during my afternoon teas. Mother thought I was crazy but I finally convinced her through my tears to take the dress across the street to the old lady's house. Mother returned a bit dazed and explained to me that our neighbor seemed thrilled to alter the dress and she would only accept a small fee for her materials. When I went later for the fitting, she had already transformed that ugly dress into a beautiful gown. I don't know how she did it. I was just glad the bow thing was gone. She never mentioned our afternoon teas, so thinking she had forgotten I never did either. I never saw her again.

Oh yeah, the fairy tale part. I went to the prom. It was the most romantic night of my life (to that point) – even though it was short. I had had to be home by eleven.

When I was in high school, in the late '60s, I had a "hippie" friend who preached love and wore peace symbols and bells around his neck. He had long hair and let his thumb nail grow out as a guitar pick. He was the only hippie in our school. I found him fascinating and everything he said captivated me. His idea of the world sounded so perfect that I believed everything he said. His motto (although not original) was, "all you need is love." He felt that if we all just loved each other everything else would work out. I bought into it completely. It wasn't long until I became guilty by association. Everyone knew we were friends and that I idolized him. One particular cynical teacher used to tease me in class about my beliefs, or rather my friend's beliefs. The teacher would say, "You can't live on love" or "how are you going to make a living on love?" He pointed out daily that you can't wear love, can't eat it, and it doesn't provide you with shelter. He was relentless in his teasing and I think he looked forward to me being in his class. I was crushed by his abuse and embarrassed because I had no defense. After all, these ideas were not really mine, although I instinctively recognized the truth in them. I was unable to defend what I knew so little about. Eventually it was too much for me to take. I didn't like being the center of attention. Sadly, I eventually let my friend go and learned to live with the cynics. It's taken me years to relearn what I knew at fifteen. All you need is love.

It seems as humans we have the most difficult time making decisions. It is true that everything we do has consequences. It is not usually possible to escape those consequences no matter how long we worry over our decisions. This I learned at a pretty young age. When I was about fifteen, I decided to break up with the boyfriend I'd had for a couple of years. He was a nice guy – but being a typical teenage girl, I was restless to date other guys and wasn't quite ready to settle for one. He, on the other hand, was quite serious about us having a future together. A few weeks before I told him my decision, he gave me an elaborate gift. He had made a model of our "dream house" out of Popsicle sticks. That may not sound like much but it was a very detailed engineering feat of a beautiful A-frame. It must have taken him many hours to put it together. He didn't take the break up well. I was very relieved with my decision – until my mother told me that I needed to return the gift. She said it wasn't right for me to keep such a gift – especially since I had accepted it knowing I was going to break up with him. I was furious with her. It meant contacting him again and I was sure he wanted me to have the house. But she insisted. I finally had to do what she thought was right. Thinking back on it now, of course she was right. I have tried to be more careful about hurting other people ever since. Every decision we make does have consequences. That doesn't mean we shouldn't make decisions or we might make the wrong ones. The important thing is how we accept those consequences and what we learn from dealing with them. That, it seems is what life is all about.

"Everything old is new again" just popped into my head one day. We know these words from an old song refer to fads and fashions coming back into style decades after they were first popular. My first thoughts were to shudder at paisley and bellbottoms, but I knew I was getting a more important message than fashion nightmares. When I was a teenager, I wrote a long and scathing entry into my diary. I was angry that my life seemed to be going in circles. I can't imagine now what made up those circles, but it is true that we keep doing the same things over and over. I have always had problems dealing with that. Every time we clean the house, it just gets dirty again. Every time we cut our hair, it grows. Every time we buy new shoes, they wear out. Our whole lives are about repeating, but we keep doing it because that's the way life is. Every time we do something again we do it a little better or faster or smarter. It should not surprise us that our spiritual challenges come in circles, too. We keep dealing with the same things over and over and never seem to "conquer" them. I don't think we're supposed to. I think we are supposed to just keep doing them better. Instead of, "oh no, here it is again" maybe we should think, "oh yes, I know this one and I can do it better this time." It will be less painful, less stressful and I will get through it much easier than I did last time, because I know more about how to do it. At one time in the seventies, my entire wardrobe was made up of paisley. Now I only have one paisley scarf, which I choose not to wear.

Anger is an emotion we all struggle with our entire lives. I'd like to say that when I was young I learned to channel my anger into constructive change, but like most people my anger still erupts unchecked at times. I was sixteen and dating a very nice boy. We'd been going out for several months when he took me aside and told me it just wasn't going to work out between us. I was dumbfounded. He said I got angry with him too often. True, if he was late for a date, or didn't call when he said, or chose to work on his car instead of spend time with me, I let him have it. I couldn't see how that was my fault. The worst part about the breakup was that it was two weeks before prom. At first, I was devastated, but then I really got angry that he would dump me right before the big event. He finally agreed to take me to the prom – after I wore him down. I expected it would be the romantic setting I needed to get us back together. He had other ideas. He took me there but spent the entire evening with some of his buddies, and left me sitting all alone. By the time he came back to take me home, I was no longer in a mood to reconcile our relationship. I was so furious with him that I never wanted to see him again! As the years have passed, I think of that situation often – every time I get angry. The Universe tried to teach me a great lesson. Anger is often about a need to control. If someone does something other than what we want, we become angry. If a situation doesn't turn out like we plan, we become angry. The alternatives are endless. Anger can be a tool to look at a person or situation in a different light – to make different choices. It can show us where our insecurities lie and how we can change ourselves to make life less stressful. One thing I know for certain is that I've never gained anything by becoming angry. I've never "won" an argument. I have no one but myself to blame for not having a good time at my high school prom. At least, I'm not angry with him anymore.

Parents try to teach their children things, but we all know that children learn the most by observation. No matter what we tell them, they will watch us and learn by what we do. That's a scary thought! When I was a teenager, I had a profound learning experience by watching my mother – when I didn't listen to a word she said. Let me back up a bit. Mother grew up at a time when a driver's license wasn't even required. Like most young people she learned to drive from her older brothers and sisters and didn't consider it a big deal. After marrying my father, she began to get out of the habit of driving. As per the norm of the time, men drove and women rode. Then her children started coming along and she stopped driving altogether. There wasn't much need for her to drive. The church, our grocery and the school were all within two blocks of the house. Even when she went back to work, she was within walking distance of her office. When my grandfather died and the grocery store was sold, Dad went to work at a factory forty miles away. He carpooled with other workers so the family car (we only ever had one) stayed in the garage much of the time. Now he wasn't nearby to fetch home groceries or run us kids to the places we needed to go. After twenty plus years, my mother decided to learn to drive again – when she was around fifty years old. It was a practical decision she thought. She could get a better job and help out and if there was an emergency, she would be able to take care of things. My father was dead set against it and refused to teach her or help her in any way. He evolved a bit later on but at that time, he was very controlling and usually vetoed most of her ideas. He could not accept any form of independence from her. Mother, however, did not back down. I remember the "discussions" well. She simply told him, in no uncertain terms, that she was going to learn to drive again and get her license whether he helped her or not. After many of these discussions and Mother beginning to study for the test, he finally relented and taught her to drive our car – grumbling all the way. That didn't seem to faze my mother. She was never a great driver and she was nervous behind the wheel, but she did it. She passed her test and used the car like everybody else for work and errands around town. She did get a better job a couple of miles from home. Even though I was a teenager and mortified by anything my parents did – secretly I was quite proud.

For all of my high school years I was in the marching band. Our band director pushed us very hard and our band won many awards. When I was sixteen, he arranged for us to march in the Orange Bowl Parade in Miami. It took months of fund raising projects to earn enough money for us to make the trip and we all worked very hard. I wasn't that thrilled about the trip. It would mean leaving home right after Christmas and being gone for a week. I had to leave my boyfriend over the holidays and, frankly, I had never traveled very far from home before so it was a daunting prospect. I still remember the goodbye at the buses and wishing I didn't have to go. I settled in as best any one could on a bus full of rowdy high school students, (there were 150 of us on three buses) and reluctantly went along for the ride. About a week before we left I had cut my thumb while opening a cat food can. I had to have stitches. It was a serous wound and I still carry the scar years later. All of the weight of an alto saxophone is carried by the right thumb. So although I was going along for the ride, I would not actually be able to play in the parade. The band director told me to just carry the sax with both hands and pretend to play. I was a rank leader and he wasn't going to let me sit this one out. I also wouldn't be able to go into the ocean on my first trip to Florida unless I secured a plastic bag over my hand. I was mortified at that prospect and refused to even entertain the idea. As the journey progressed and I became more and more depressed something strange began to happen. I noticed all the new and unusual things outside my bus window such as palm trees and orange groves. We stopped at Cypress Gardens and toured the paradise there and my spirits began to lift a bit. When we got to Miami, I found it was a beautiful city. I'd never seen anything like it before. We saw the mansions of Miami Beach and finally the ocean itself in all of its power and glory. I remember the moment when I was finally alone in my hotel room (shared with three other teenage girls). A sense of wonder seeped over me at every new experience I had recently had (I'd never stayed in a motel before) and I realized that the world was bigger and more wondrous than I had ever imagined it from my small Indiana town. I don't remember the parade at all. I'm sure it was hard work and I think we did okay. I do remember sitting on the beach, with my plastic bag over my hand and deciding that since I was there, I was going to go into that water and I no longer cared about embarrassment. I remember the feeling of awe that awakened in me on that trip. I came home knowing deep within that there would always be more to life than I could ever imagine.

When I was about seventeen years old, the boy I was dating invited me to his sister's home for a tree trimming party. Their whole family was there and they had food and sang Christmas songs while they all shared in decorating a beautiful tree. It was a wondrous night for me. I had never experienced anything like it. In my family, unfortunately, trimming the tree had always turned into a struggle between my parents as they argued about how and what was to be done. My dad cursed the tangle of lights and complained because my mother couldn't make up her mind which direction she wanted the tree to face. My mother wasn't very artistic and the tree, with its faded and chipped decorations always ended up a bit lopsided and frankly looked pathetic. Year after year, I had witnessed this ritual in disappointment. When I got home from the party that night, my parents had left the Christmas tree lights on in the living room. This was not something they usually did when they went to bed. They left them on – just for me. I started to reach for the switch to flip them off but something went through me. To this day, I'm not sure what it was, but I smiled and sat down on the couch and just stared at our pathetic little tree twinkling in the darkness for a very long time.

There are so many rules that we live by. Some of these rules are imposed upon us by our parents, our bosses, the government and many other institutions. But the rules that are most harmful to us, I believe, are the rules we impose upon ourselves. We do things according to a set of beliefs and often do not realize the limits and the consequences it brings. My parents were big on rules. They both got very uncomfortable when any rule was broken, so I grew up trying very hard not to put myself in a situation that went against their rules – at least not so they noticed. My mother had Alzheimer's disease for the last fifteen years of her life and was even showing symptoms when I was still a teenager. Although she lived until I was forty, she was really "gone" by the time I was in my late twenties. I never got to know her as an adult. She was so strict when I was little. They both ruled with uncompromising authority.

When I was about seventeen, my steady boyfriend was getting ready to leave for basic training. He was going to be gone a few months. I was still in high school and he worked second shift at a factory in a neighboring town so we only saw each other on weekends. He was leaving early on a Saturday morning and I wanted to see him one more time before he left. I couldn't see any way that would happen. My curfew was 11:00 on Friday nights and he didn't get off work until 12:30 – and was thirty minutes away. I appealed to my older sister who was home from college. She suggested that she take me to meet him after his work. We could meet at the service station owned by her boyfriend's family. We could see each other a few minutes at least, but it would mean sneaking out of the house and back in again – long after a curfew that I had never before broken. She was twenty two and had no curfew.

I don't know what made me risk it but I went to my mother with the plan, hoping to beg for permission. She thought for a moment and looked at me carefully, and then said okay. I was shocked. She had never before bent, let alone, broken any rule. She said that I was not to tell my father and we would have to be very quiet about it so he did not find out. She didn't get any argument from me. The night came. My sister and I were quiet as mice and got away safely. I had a brief goodbye with my boyfriend and it really meant a lot to both of us to see each other that night. I guess with all the euphoria of our successful espionage, my sister and I were a little careless coming back into the house. I heard Dad moving around and knew he was awake and we'd been caught. We rushed upstairs to our room and waited for the boom to fall. Although I heard my parents arguing for a while, no one ever came upstairs. When the morning came, Dad left for work as always and nothing was said. My mother acted totally normal. I wasn't about to ask questions. If she hadn't broken the rules just that once, I would never have known that my mother would take a fall for me. I never would have known that she understood my romantic schoolgirl notions and respected my need to see my boyfriend before he left. I never would have known that she trusted me. I am so grateful now for that glimpse into the relationship we might have had when I grew up.

When I first heard about the concept of detachment I thought, just like everybody does, that it meant we had to give up our stuff. That idea seemed a little odd to me although ascetics have chosen it for centuries. Why would we be in a universe of plenty only to have to deny ourselves having any of it?

Recently, I was thinking back to my teen years. I was among the generation that cruised the streets on weekend nights from one hamburger joint to another. It was an elaborate mating ritual, really. The coolest boys usually drove alone in souped up, jacked up hot rods. The girls ran in packs. We'd fit as many in a car, usually our father's, as possible. There were two drive-in restaurants at either end of the main strip through town. The restaurant on the south end of the strip was the best. The building sat perpendicular to the highway and there were two rows of parking attended by car hops. Cars circled the rows in a continuous stream every night. We didn't always eat but there was a rule that to park you had to order something. We could make a soda last all night long! Once we got a prime place to park we didn't want to lose it! A few years earlier, my sister first spotted her husband while she was sitting in that back row. He cruised by in his 1966 yellow Plymouth Satellite and that was it for her. There was always one guy who was the king of the night. He had the best car and all the girls swooned when he drove by. Everyone dreamed of riding in that car with him. I remember the guy who was "it" for a couple of years when I was in high school. Like all the girls I thought he was really cool. We all just held our breath waiting for a nod or look from him to come our way. The problem with this restaurant was that it sat on a four lane highway. To leave the cruising area it was necessary to pull left into oncoming traffic. Sometimes it took forever to pull out.

I remember sitting in the line a few cars behind "him" that night. After he drove by a lot of us pulled out to follow him. We were all giggling and carrying on as usual. Suddenly, I heard a sickening noise I'd never heard before. It was metal crashing hard into metal. We opened our doors and flew out of our car and saw that his car had been hit hard in the side. Everything stopped. Soon the ambulance arrived and his car was pushed out of the way and the night went on as usual. I never saw him again. I did hear that he survived and made it to his graduation in a wheelchair. I don't remember his name. I didn't then know anything about him except that he had the coolest car. I do remember what his car looked like. Soon there was another guy in another great car who took his place. But I realized something that night when I looked at his crumpled up car. He was his car to all of us. Never again would he be in the position of most desired guy in town. It was years before I knew what that meant.

When we identify strongly with any material thing, it replaces the concept of our true self. That is what is wrong with our attachment to things. If we think we are our car, or our job, or relationship, or the clothes we wear, or even the persona we portray, then those things become more important than who we really are. We lose ourselves in the process. In an instant, any of those things can be taken away. Then who are we? It is not about what we have. It is about our attachment to what we think makes us. So enjoy your stuff. Have plenty of it! Just know that it is not you.

Why can't we change other people? Why, when we know what will make them happier, when we know what would improve our relationship with them won't the Universe allow us to inflict our will? For me, this desire to change others, started early in life with my mother. She never quite measured up to what I thought a mother should be like. She wasn't beautiful or particularly loving or understanding. She was a product of the 40s and 50s. For most of my childhood, she was a housewife, but she was no June Cleaver. She was not the "hip" mother all the kids in the neighborhood loved. She was usually angry and frustrated. She seemed to detest housework, became upset at the slightest provocation and preached her morality until I found myself avoiding contact with her whenever possible. I wanted her to be different. I wanted her to comfort me when I cried. I believed she didn't love me. She didn't handle the challenges of motherhood too well and I often wondered why my sisters and I were part of her life at all. My relationship with Mother became guarded and superficial. Mother, as a child and a young woman was a writer, a performer, and an independent thinker. These were qualities unheard of for a woman in her time. When she married, she gave up herself to be what she was supposed to be – a wife and mother. That made her very unhappy. Over the years, she grew more and more away from herself and molded her life to be what was expected of her. By the time I was born, when Mother was thirty-five, there was very little left of the vivacious, free spirit that graduated high school at age sixteen. When I was a child, I could not accept Mother the way she was. I cried many tears. I wanted her to be different. I wanted her to be the type of mother I wanted her to be. Of course, I could not understand then that Mother was doing the best she could. My mother became afflicted with Alzheimer's when I was still in my twenties. She was no longer the woman I remembered or that spirited child that died before I was born. If I could have changed her then, I would have loved her to be just like she was while I was growing up, instead of the empty shell she became. Her personality was gone completely. There was no chance to recapture a little spark and fan it into a life. I could not change what this disease had done. I could not change the choices Mother made to lead her to this point. My mother, whatever she was or wasn't, was gone. I could not change her anymore than I could have when I was a child. No one could. If it is within your power, within your heart, tell someone you love them just the way they are – while they can still hear you.

SECTION THREE

The mistakes of others always look bigger

and messier than our own.

If I had to use one word to describe my childhood, it would be "sheltered." Not only sheltered by my parents, but by the entire environment in which I grew up. Everyone in my community was of the same race. Everyone I played with belonged to the same church my family did. Words like sex, beer and even darn were strictly taboo. The real hippies were way off in California and I didn't understand Janis Joplin. Then suddenly at age 17, I was plummeted into another world – college. The cultural shock was many-faceted. One of the things which struck me first was the variety of people. I was taught to fear those who were different and to avoid contact whenever possible. Sadly, bigotry had been as common as corn fields my first seventeen years. Was I a bigot? I honestly didn't know. I was curious about others but apprehensive about being in social settings with those who were unlike me.

I remember the first time I was alone with someone of a different race. I had been studying in the lobby of the dorm. Instead of going back to my wing to the rest room, I wandered through the halls until I found one nearer to the lobby. I barged through the door and came face to face with a young black girl about my age. I froze. She was washing her hands and she looked up at me and smiled. "Hi," she said. I think I said hi back, but I honestly can't remember. She brushed past me and that was that. My knees were still shaking.

After that, I stayed pretty much on my own turf. I was dating and having fun. Serious thoughts were rare in those days because I was so busy soaking up all of life. In February, I became engaged. I was so excited to show off my ring to the girls on my wing. My roommate told me that another girl in the dorm had become engaged on Valentine's Day too, and was also showing off a ring. She encouraged me to go with her to visit the other girl. "You guys can compare notes," she said. She thought we would have so much to talk about. It sounded like fun, so I followed her to the other side of the dorm. The girl's door was open and we could hear excited squeals coming from within. There were lots of girls milling around. As we entered, my roommate said, "This is Sue and she just got engaged too!" The crowd parted and there on the bed sat the girl from the bathroom. Oh boy, I thought. She smiled as she had the first time and held out her left hand. Her ring was antique, quite different from my solitaire but it was beautiful. I held mine out, too. She took my hand and invited me to sit beside her. I did and she started talking. She asked me if I had set the date, was I going to have a big wedding, was I going to stay in school? As I answered her questions, I started asking my own. We both wanted simple but pretty ceremonies, we both secretly planned to drop out of school. We both worried that our boyfriends would be sent to Vietnam.

I left her room that afternoon knowing that she and I were more alike than different. And knowing that she was not what I had been afraid of, but rather, the horrible monster of bigotry. I am still afraid of it, because I see it so often in others. I know it does not exist within me. I never saw her again. She eloped and left school. They say masters touch in with us every now and then - to teach us a special lesson.

While I was still in college, I got my first Siamese cat. His name was J.C. and true to the breed, he was quite a character. My parents had never allowed animals in the house – let alone in our beds so I was of the opinion that animals should not sleep with me. J.C. was very persistent and no matter how many times I pushed him off the bed, he always came back and tried to snuggle in. Finally, I got the brilliant idea that if he had his own special bed, I could sleep cat free. I bought him a very nice wooden bed with velvety cushions and put it at the foot of my bed. I gently placed him in the bed and he just kept walking out. Over and over again we repeated this routine. I was of a mind that persistence would eventually pay off. After several weeks of this, I realized that J.C. was never going to lie down in that bed, let alone sleep in it. And he never did. After about a year, I sold the bed at a yard sale. I think of J.C. often. I really loved that cat. I think of him when someone is doing something that I would really like to change. No matter how persistent I have been, I never have changed anyone's behavior. Not really. The desire to change others is always futile. I learned to accept J.C. in my bed. That was who he was. My only other option was to shut him out of the bedroom and listen to him cry at the door. I guess we can shut people out of our lives when we don't like what they do, too. Or, just maybe we could learn to change ourselves instead. Maybe we can accept others exactly as they are and see what happens. For me, I learned that in the middle of the night when I wake up with a bad dream, there's a little cat face purring on my shoulder and the bad dream melts away. It's not J.C. anymore, of course. He's running things somewhere in the afterlife, I'm sure.

Every year, my first husband and I hosted a Halloween party at our lake house. J.C. was used to our parties, and came and went as if nothing unusual was going on. One year, a friend of ours arrived at the party riding a horse! He was dressed as a cowboy or some such thing. Anyway, as the horse came down the long gravel driveway, he did what horses do. Toward the end of the evening I was looking around for J.C. and spotted him out in the driveway furiously trying to cover up the horse's "mistake." Gravel was flying in all directions as he worked at his monumental task. The pile was as big as J.C. – no way could he successfully cover it. It occurs to me now that J.C. wasn't that great at covering his own "piles" in the litter box. He was always too lazy or too busy to take the time. I usually had to do it for him. Why was he so obsessed with this job? I guess the mistakes of others always look bigger and messier than our own.

One of the things my ex-husband used to say all the time was "you get what you pay for." He said it to the point of driving me crazy. He was a third generation owner of a furniture and appliance store. It would drive him crazy when people would buy cheap furniture and then complain about the quality or cut corners on a major appliance that would break down after a short period of time. He always tried to talk customers into buying the best they could afford – not because it was a better sale for him but just because it didn't make sense to do otherwise. Obviously many people didn't agree with his philosophy and bought the cheapest item available, and then complained when it didn't satisfy their expectations. He hammered it in to me for fifteen years that if I bought something cheap, I got something cheap. Being a born bargain hunter, I must confess I gave him ample opportunities to say "I told you so." The other day, his words appeared in my head again as they do from time to time. I started playing with the idea that we truly do always get exactly what we pay for. Whatever effort, energy, passion or dedication we pay out determines the quality of our entire lives. Whatever we are willing to give in love, compassion and friendship is what we end up having. If we cut corners, or try to find a way around paying the price, we are never satisfied with what we have. I'm thinking maybe that he was right. We shouldn't complain about what we have if we have exactly what we paid for.

When my parents were married, it wasn't a fancy affair. They drove to Indianapolis on a Sunday afternoon and Mother's brother, a Methodist minister, performed the ceremony in his home. His wife was the only witness. It was 1938 and my parents had no money. When they came home, Mother moved into her in-laws' home while Dad's uncles built the house they lived in for fifty five years. It wasn't exactly a fairy tale beginning and they didn't have a fairy tale marriage – from what I observed. They struggled with just about every conceivable obstacle along the way and often were at odds against one another. I have often wondered about the endurance of their union. It was partly a product of the times, I think, but also it was a commitment that is rarely seen between people these days. Mother didn't believe in divorce and she once told my sister that in a marriage there were green times and brown times. During the brown times, you endured until the green times came around again. At the time, both my sister and I thought the analogy was rather stupid, but maybe there was something to it after all. Now I'm not advocating staying in a marriage that is unhealthy or destructive, but I do think that staying for a lifetime with one person must offer numerous opportunities to learn and grow. Often we ditch relationships just when the true growth could occur and end up having the same issues with someone new. It never pays to give up on anything too quickly, especially during times of stress. It just could be the time when we will ascend to a new level of awareness, which could also bring about a new level of relationship.

I used to be so afraid of storms. They are so powerful and there is just no way to escape their fury. Every cloudy day I would watch the sky and worry about what might happen. On April 3, 1974, the worst storms in a long time hit Louisville and Southern Indiana with a vengeance. Lives were lost, property destroyed and many people lost everything they had, their possessions scattered over several counties. On that day I was living near a little town in Indiana that was one of the places hardest hit. The tornados came with very little warning just as the school children were being released for the day. I had let my cat outside about one that afternoon. Now, J.C. was basically a house cat but every once in a while he liked to wander around and play hunter in the woods. He rarely stayed gone too long and then he would come to the door, demand entrance and head for my bed. When the skies suddenly became dark, I began calling for J.C., but he did not come. I stood at the patio doors and called through the hail, the eerie quiet, the pouring rain, and the wind. J.C. did not come. Because the power went out, I wasn't aware of how bad the storm was just a few miles from my home. I was so worried. I had to go out for a few hours that night to meet my parents at a movie their church was showing. I didn't want to leave home not knowing J.C.'s fate. I had promised I would go and I couldn't get out of it. I left the patio door cracked open just a hair. It wasn't until I got with other people that I heard how devastating the tornados had been. The National Guard had been activated and my parents were so worried about relatives who lived in a near-by town. The phone lines were down and there was no way to get any news. Through it all, I kept thinking about J.C. A poor little defenseless cat! He couldn't possibly have survived alone, outside. I went home that night thinking I was right to fear spring and the unpredictable weather it brings. Disaster was all around me. Fortunately, my home and family were safe and, although I watched the entire storm from the open patio doors, I was safe too. The house was dark. It would be three days before electricity was restored. I went to the dining room and slid the patio doors shut with a sigh, lit a candle and made my way to the bedroom. There, curled in a ball, sound asleep was my precious J.C.

He was dry, unhurt and he griped when I hugged him, same as always. How in the world did he come through all of the chaos completely unhurt, I wondered? His instincts must have allowed him to find someplace safe to hide. Or maybe it wasn't his time to leave me, so he survived. All the fear and worry in the world doesn't change how things will be. I'm not afraid of storms anymore.

In the mid-1970s I was returning home from a trip to Washington, D.C. Washington, with its hundreds of stone monuments and endless array of government buildings, had disappointed me. Bureaucracy floated through the air like a cold drifting snow. I had never developed a feel for my country's history or pride. Perhaps growing up in the Vietnam era had dampened my sense of patriotism. Somewhere in the middle of Virginia, a road sign caught my eye. Monticello, next exit. It wouldn't hurt to see one more president's home. It was time to take a driving break anyway. As the car exited the highway, I could see the Blue Ridge Mountains rising in the distance. The colors of thousands of trees covered by an ever-present mist began to warm me. Monticello is the Italian word for little mountain. The car groaned up and around that little mountain through untouched forests. A red brick house mastered the summit. Its white domed roof and massive columns gleamed in the sunlight. Inside, each room was filled with books, gadgets and inventions. Each window viewed a unique garden, carefully planned by the president, himself. He kept a record of each time a flower bloomed and the precise moment each one died. He was just a name in the history books to me. I discovered that he was the founder of the University of Virginia and architect of its magnificent buildings. He was author of the first State Statute of Religious Freedom, the second Ambassador to France, first Secretary of State, second Vice President and third President of the United States. He was the author of "We hold these truths to be self evident, that all men are created equal." Maybe I should look at those history books again. Who was this man who read Latin, French, Italian, Spanish and Greek and studied Sir Isaac Newton, Francis Bacon and John Locke? I felt like I knew him. I was sure I had. Monticello felt so familiar to me. I knew the house, each room. I knew the land as I made my way to his grave, where I stood and wept. In some other time, perhaps in some other life, I'd been this way before.

Does the thought of the holidays send dread or joy into your heart? I think for most people the holidays are a mixture of dread and joy. Yes, there are definitely some obligations that have to be fulfilled. But if there are more obligations than moments of pleasure, the holidays are not doing what they were designed to do: give us a break from our ordinary lives and remind us of how blessed we are. Years ago, some friends and I were talking. The holidays were fast approaching. We were all commiserating about how much we dreaded this or that. Then someone got an idea. I'd like to think it was me but I honestly don't remember. Why don't we make our own holiday? We did just that. We got together slightly before the official holiday season with just friends and (desired) family, cooked only what we wanted, bought presents for each other because we chose to (or not), dressed the way we wanted and had a great time. There were no expectations, no hurt feelings, no games or manipulations. In fact, no baggage at all. We called it our real Christmas. It made all the obligatory holiday activities bearable. We continued our tradition for several years until life sent us in different directions. It's not enough just to rebel and say you won't do this or that anymore. Because then, your focus is on what you don't like and the balance goes the wrong way. Your holidays will end up miserable. Remember, there must always be a balance. That's all there is to it. Do what you have to do and do what you want to do and make them compliment each other. I guarantee that your holiday attitude will improve and your stress level will go way down.

Back in the 1970s, my sister and I owned a framing store and gallery. Besides custom framing, we also carried signed prints and art, sculpture and ceramics and other decorating items. One day, a lady came into our store. She was very well dressed, nice and pleasant. She told us that she was a floral designer and would be interested in placing some of her pieces in our store on consignment. She described her work in detail. We hadn't carried floral arrangements in the store before, but inventory was a bit low and we thought her work might be a nice addition to our stock. She was thrilled and promised to bring about a dozen pieces in the following day. She did. When we saw what she brought in, we were shocked. The arrangements looked like what is left after a cat has played with them (I know about that). The silk flowers were stuck into exposed clay with no shape or design or even complimentary colors. The pots were cheap and dirty and obviously reused. She chatted on about her work, so proud and excited that we were speechless. She left her pieces and trotted out the door. We had a problem. We didn't want to put them in our store! We also didn't want to hurt the lady's feelings by telling her to come back and get them. My sister, who'd worked for a florist, straightened up the best two and we put the others in a back room. After about a month one piece actually sold. We called the woman and she came in. We told her at that time that we no longer had room to carry her flowers and she was gracious and ended our agreement. My sister and I discussed for a long time how deluded the woman was. Now I'm not so sure. Yes her arrangements were ugly. But we were not the only store to carry them. She had them all over town and from what she told us, they sold quite well. What was going on here? I think she believed in her work. I think from her perspective she was a floral artist and by representing herself as such she actually got stores to carry her work – like us. I think from her perspective it was a very successful venture. I think, with the right perspective, anything must be possible.

Years ago, a friend of mine was going through a particularly bad time. She was very disappointed in her life and she used to say if she never expected anything, she would never be disappointed. It's a slight twist on a quote by Alexander Pope. At the time, I thought that was a horrible way to feel – having no positive expectations for the future. That may have been exactly the way she meant it. But when I think about that phrase now, I see it a bit differently. Usually, what we expect in life is determined by our very narrow viewpoint of what life can give. We expect certain things to happen (a new love, a new job or whatever) and when they don't we blame the Universe for letting us down. We expect those things to come about exactly the way we envision them. The Universe has a scope much broader than that. If we don't expect anything then we don't limit what blessings may come to us and from what avenue they may reach us. What we envision for ourselves may be far less than the Universe has in store for us. While we're dreaming of a particular job or particular mate, the perfect job or the perfect mate may be beyond our scope of manifestation. The Universe is waiting for us to let go of our limited viewpoint and accept unlimited possibilities.

Election seasons are longer than ever. The campaigning seems to go on and on. It may be that many of us get so tired of it that we don't even make a trip to the polls. Not so with me. You see, I could never skip an election. Something bad would happen, like a rain of toads or something. It was instilled in me at a very young age that I must always vote. My mother wasn't necessarily political. I mean, she never ran for office or even worked for a candidate that I know of. She always made certain she was very informed about the issues. She would read everything she could get her hands on about each candidate, no matter what the office. No one ever knew who she voted for. She was adamant about her right to not disclose her vote. Dad always just joked that she cancelled out his votes every year. In a world where women didn't yet have many rights, she always took this one very seriously. My sisters and I were always expected to vote. She even arranged for me to vote absentee when I was away at college. Each election, she volunteered to work at the polls and put in a long day until every vote was counted. The last time she worked an election was not too long after we were aware that Alzheimer's disease was taking its toll on her. Dad worried about taking her that year but she insisted upon going. In a very short while one of the other workers called him to come and pick Mother up. She was no longer capable of doing what she had done for many years. And, she had forgotten to vote. So I will vote. I will always vote. Not so much because I'm passionate about one candidate or another, but because I can.

I didn't like Thanksgiving much as a child or young adult. It was a day I was forced to spend at my parents' home, bored, with Mother stressed out over a dinner that always took too long to get to the table and wasn't always a culinary delight. The only good thing about Thanksgiving was that it was a prelude to Christmas. I knew that very early in life. It took commerce a little longer to figure it out. Today we begin celebrating Christmas before Thanksgiving has even arrived. One year, I had the opportunity to go out of town on business instead of spending Thanksgiving with my family. I jumped at the chance. I wouldn't have to face a combination of idiosyncrasies and personalities I could only marginally tolerate. The holiday itself meant nothing to me. I went on my trip and ended up driving home through Chicago on Thanksgiving Day. Everything was cool, no problems and I didn't miss anyone or anything. The by-pass had these strange rest stops that included restaurants over the interstate. Good enough place for Thanksgiving dinner, I thought. When I walked into the restaurant a peculiar feeling hit the pit of my stomach. It wasn't hunger. The place was practically deserted. The only food available was cold sandwiches. I suppose most of the employees had the day off to be with their families. I began to feel lonely then, but I couldn't figure out why. I choked down the food and continued on my way. The rest of the trip got worse and worse. Depression really hit hard late that evening when I passed through the town where my sister lived. My family had spent the day there. All, except me. I missed Thanksgiving that year. I mean, I really missed it. Christmas came right on schedule, but something just wasn't right. As Christmas keeps getting pushed earlier and earlier maybe some day it will make it a full year ahead, back to December 25th were it belongs and Thanksgiving can be a special time again, as it deserves. A time to be thankful for the bountiful harvest of life. Part of that bounty is family.

I believe one of the hardest jobs in this life is parenting. I often wonder why we are not required to undergo rigorous schooling and testing before being given the power to guide other human beings during the beginning of their journeys on this earth. What we do and how we do it in raising our kids makes the difference in the future of each one of them and the entire planet. So many people take this as a second job. I'm not talking about working parents. In our society today, most of us must work at jobs to survive, to give our children even the minimal advantages they require to grow into the best people they can be. We often use our jobs, however, or the way our parents raised us or many other excuses to lighten our responsibility as parents. Since there is no training for this most important job, oftentimes, despite our best efforts as parents, we feel we have failed. Is there really anything we can do, any guidelines to insure success with our children? Of course not. We are dealing with people here. Little people with individual souls and personalities and their own karma to be worked out. We can't insure success, but we can tip the scales in our favor. Several years before my daughter was born I was making plans with a friend on a Saturday morning. She matter-of-factly told me that she couldn't leave the house until after a certain time because her son had a favorite cartoon show he enjoyed each week. After all, she said, she and her husband had special things they enjoyed that did not include their son and he had the same right to enjoy his favorite show. This was before TV shows could be recorded, so the program could not be watched later. I was so impressed that they respected their young son in that way. This was a new concept for me: respecting children as individuals, trying to understand their needs, and giving them rights. It was such a simple thing, and far different from the way I had been raised. I never forgot it. My daughter was not a perfect child. No human being is. I received many compliments on her behavior and her respect for others as she was growing up. I based my parenting philosophy on the lesson I learned from my friend before my daughter was born. After all, you get back whatever you put out. It's not a guarantee for success, but it's a start.

When my holiday tradition with friends started years ago, we picked the Sunday before Christmas and I volunteered to serve as host. I had never prepared a holiday meal all by myself, since every holiday occasion until that time had been spent at my parents' house. I thought I could handle it. How hard could it be? The first recipe I searched for was Wassail. I wanted a hot beverage to serve to my guests as they arrived on a cold December day. The recipe I finally settled on was the one we still enjoy today. I also volunteered to bake a turkey and my friends were to bring the side dishes and desserts. On that Sunday morning, I was up early making sure the house and all the trimmings were just right. I had bought a beautiful punch bowl to set in the middle of the dining room table. It was just perfect for the Wassail. I put the turkey in the oven to bake, following the very simple instructions. Right before the time the guests were to arrive, I poured the steaming hot Wassail into the bowl. I turned back toward the kitchen and heard an awful sound! The bowl had exploded and the punch was running all over my beautiful table and down onto the floor. It was so sticky and littered with glass! I thought I'd never get it cleaned up in time. It was the 70s and there was light green shag carpet beneath that table that matted together as if it had been glued!

Finally, I was satisfied that no one would even know of the catastrophe and I quickly covered the table with another cloth and reset the places. I had bought extra ingredients in case I needed another batch of the Wassail. As my guests arrived, I was still able to hand them a hot cup of punch. Fastest cleaning job I ever did! No one was the wiser. At the appointed time, I went to take the turkey out of the oven. It not only wasn't done it was still cold! I couldn't figure out what I'd done wrong. I pulled one of my guests aside who was an experienced cook. She pointed out that I'd left the giblet package inside the turkey! At that point I broke down and confessed my folly to all of my guests. I was devastated but they only laughed. One dear friend suggested I just make another pot of Wassail and we'd happily wait for the turkey to finish cooking. I did and the Wassail saved the day! I learned three very important lessons that day. Never pour hot liquid into a glass punch bowl. Always search a turkey for hidden parts. And most important, real friends don't judge, especially if there is enough Wassail in the house! I would not attempt a holiday party without it – just in case!

Very few people go through their lives without some time or another being owned by a pet. Oh, there are people who claim not to like animals, but it is usually the responsibility and inevitability of loss that turns them off. Pets are friends who never judge, criticize or disappoint. They are always loyal and only ask for love, a kind word, or a rub on the tummy. When they are gone, the loss can be overwhelming. J.C., my Seal Point Siamese cat thought he was the King of Siam. For ten years, he dominated my household. His grace and beauty was unmatched by anything human. He could leap effortlessly to the top of the bookcases or tiptoe across the I-beam in the basement without disturbing the dust. He never made a mess, never broke anything. He could unravel a whole ball of yarn and tangle it through the furniture in every room in the house while I was gone to the grocery. He would sit on a little blue chair in the bathroom each morning while I put on my make-up and sleep at my feet each night. I loved him and he loved me. Every time I sat down, he was on my lap, kneading my leg and purring. Sometimes, I sat down just to accommodate him because holding him was so important. When my daughter was just a few months old, J.C. fell off a window ledge in the basement and died. It was such a shock, the way it happened. He had his own pet door in the window and he came and went through it daily for most of his life. But that day, he fell. I knew what had happened. The child had replaced J.C. as first in my affections. I was busy and for the first time there was a room in the house in which he wasn't allowed. The cat chose not to exist as second best. I missed J.C. I got other cats shortly after he died, but none compared. They weren't as smart, as personable – they all acted like cats, bringing vile presents to the back door or stealing thawing steaks off the kitchen counter. Those were things J.C. would never have done. One day when my daughter was about three, she came running to me all excited. "Mommy, Mommy. Come see the kitty," she said.

"What kitty, Joy?" I asked, knowing my cats had all been banished to the outside (we lived in the country).

"The white kitty, Mommy. On the little blue chair."

I ran to the bathroom and looked at the chair. I saw nothing, but I could feel a familiar presence. I turned and hugged my daughter.

"There was a kitty, mommy," she said.

"I know, sweetie, thank you for telling Mommy."

When I knew that my first marriage was going to end, there were still a lot of details to work out. I didn't have a lot of resources at that time and I was scared. It was what I wanted but that didn't make it any easier. I doubted myself and questioned everything in my world. Divorce wasn't common in my family. It was not something to be taken lightly. Very early in the process – we hadn't even separated yet – I was in the bathroom one morning, putting on my makeup. We lived in the country so the window was wide open to the side yard and woods beyond. I caught movement out of the corner of my eye and glanced up to the window. I saw one of the most beautiful creatures I've ever seen. She was a totally white doe. I'd never seen an albino deer before and for a minute I was frozen in time as she just gazed into my eyes. My husband was in another room and I slowly backed out of the bathroom to call him to look. When he got there, she was gone. He went outside and looked around but there was no sign of any deer anywhere. With all the stress I was under, I supposed I had just imagined her there. It didn't boost my confidence that I was now having hallucinations! But I tried to take it as a sign of encouragement. She was so beautiful and peaceful. Maybe it was just a dream to remind me to be less anxious and more positive about the future. And yet… it was an illusion. I was depressed for several days after this incident. One day I picked up the mail, which included the local newspaper. There on the front page was a picture of my deer!

Someone else in the neighborhood had seen her and been able to capture her picture. She looked just as she had outside my bathroom window.

She wasn't an illusion after all. She was rare and special, but she was real. Somehow I knew that everything was going to be alright.

Friendship is a very complicated thing. Some friendships last a very short time, like your college roommate. Some last for a lifetime. The length of time a friendship lasts does not make it necessarily better. Some people I have known for a very short time have changed my life. And sometimes, I meet someone and instantly know I could trust them with my life – and deep dark secrets. A few years ago, I almost missed the opportunity for a friendship like that because I was not open to new possibilities. I was taking meditation classes once a week in a neighboring town. At that time I lived about twenty-five miles from where the classes were held and shared a ride with a life-long friend. We used the driving time to catch up on gossip, discuss how we felt about everything we were learning in class, and share our innermost feelings about our lives. I looked forward to those talks as much as I did the classes. After a short time, the teacher told us that someone new was joining our class who lived near us. She suggested we get in touch with her to share rides. Yuck! I hated the idea of a stranger riding with us.

We wouldn't be able to talk. I was really disappointed. There seemed to be no gracious way out of it. The first night she rode with us, I liked her. I couldn't help it. She was so easy to talk to and so friendly. Within a couple of weeks, I realized that she was loving and giving and it wasn't long before I relaxed into a new friendship. We had a lot in common and she was very wise. By the time she had ridden with us about a month, I couldn't imagine my life without her. What if I had listened to my closed mindedness and not allowed her to join us or refused to open up to her? I know now that my life would be so different today without the support, advice and love of this very special person. She helped me through some hard times and always delighted in my happiness. She's been gone now for over ten years, but the friendship she gave me will last my lifetime.

SECTION FOUR

Maybe perspective is all that matters.

Once upon a time, there was a beautiful fairy princess. She lived in a castle way up on a hill. The castle was filled with many beautiful things but the fairy princess was very unhappy. She was lonely. She had so much love to give but no one special to share it with and she longed to be loved. One day, the fairy princess was sitting at the bottom of the hill, staring at her reflection in the moat and sighing. Suddenly another figure appeared at her side and she saw a reflection of green in the water. "Who are you?" she said, turning to look.

"I am a frog," he said, "and I love you."

"How can that be?" she asked. "You don't even know me."

"I know you," he said, "and I love you."

"But you're a frog and I am a fairy princess," she began.

"I know what I am," said the frog.

"What would people think – a fairy princess and a frog?!"

"I love you," said the frog patiently.

"You cannot love me. And I could never let myself love a frog. It just isn't done," she cried.

"I love you," responded the frog.

"But my friends, my family, they would never accept a frog," she said.

"I love you," he said.

"It could never work out. Not in a million years," the fairy princess said slowly. "Could it?"

She looked into the eyes of the frog – eyes filled with love, loyalty and understanding.

"I love you," he said again.

The fairy princess looked away from the frog and buried her face in her hands. Through her tears, in halting sobs she finally said, "I love, you too. And that is all that matters, isn't it?"

When the frog didn't answer she slowly took her hands away from her face, fearing he was gone. But he was there and what she saw was not a frog at all, but the most handsome prince she had ever seen, standing before her with outstretched arms.

By the time my first husband and I separated, we had really been apart for years. There is no one to blame. I have come to the conclusion that if more than one person is involved in anything, there is always responsibility on all parts. If I had to blame anything, I think I would choose immaturity. We were both so immature and selfish. Patterns were set up that we didn't know how to change. I was the one who finally said it had to end. We were living in a world where all we did was hurt each other. It had to stop. That was what I really couldn't live with anymore. I didn't want to be alone. I come from an era of romance and happy endings. I wanted that so badly. Most of all I wanted to be loved, really loved, unconditionally and forever. One night, fueled by loneliness and a bit of despair, I lit a candle and prayed to the Universe to send me someone who would love me. That was all I asked for. There were no conditions or restrictions, but the appeal was very emotional and came from the bottom of my soul. I was exhausted from the effort. Months rolled by and I continued to prepare myself for a life on my own. Then I met Ben. We became friends. I didn't expect anything else from the relationship because he was younger than me. When he first told me that he loved me, I don't think I even took him seriously. Then he gave me a tape recording and asked me to listen to it. I took it home and put it in the player and sat down at my kitchen table. It was filled with beautiful love songs he had recorded because they expressed how he felt about me. Throughout he talked over the songs and expressed those same feelings. As I sat there and listened, I remembered my prayer to the Universe. I thought, could this be? By the end of the tape, I knew I had to take the chance. It wasn't easy. A lot of people judged us. Some people exited our lives. But as we happily approach our twenty fifth wedding anniversary, all I can say is, be careful what you ask for. You just might get it.

Although my grandmother was nice to me, and okay as a grandmother, the one thing I remember most about her is that she was a worrier. Grandma worried about everything. It got to the point where my mother wouldn't tell her about our family's everyday problems because Grandma would call a dozen times to check up. She would call every hour on the hour when my sisters or I went out somewhere to see if we had made it home safely. I know how useless worry is and I never considered myself to be as bad as Grandma, but maybe it did skip a generation and land square in my lap. When I decided to file for divorce from my first husband, one of the things which worried me most was telling my father. My parents had been married for fifty years and divorces weren't commonplace in my family. My mother had already been stricken with Alzheimer's Disease and I knew she would not comprehend the situation. I was terrified how Dad would react. I remembered his wrath as a teenager. I practiced for days just what I would say and worried myself into permanent residency in the bathroom. Finally, I could stand it no longer and I had to tell him. My daughter, Joy and I went to their home for lunch. I felt tiny as I sat in Dad's overstuffed chair and said, "I'm getting a divorce." My father was doing the dishes and he stopped in mid-swipe, turned and looked at me and said, "Finally. How can I help?" You would think I would have learned my lesson? Oh, no. About a year and a half later, Ben and I decided to get married. I was afraid, once again, to tell Dad. I knew he had become so protective of me since the divorce and I was afraid of his reaction. I practiced for days to find just the right words. I was so worried, I was detracting from my happiness. One day when he came to my apartment, I knew I could put it off no longer. We sat down in my living room; I took a deep breath and shakily said that I had some news. As I think back now, I realize my father had a peculiar look on his face, sort of a smirk. I rushed on with, "Ben and I are getting married." He said, "That's not news to me. Joy told me about it a couple of weeks ago." He went on to assure me that all he cared about was my happiness. Worry is a useless emotion. Nothing is ever as bad as the energy wasted worrying over it. Worrying doesn't change the final outcome one bit. Most of the time what we worry about never takes place. Sounds like I learned this lesson? I'm not sure, I still worry about it.

When my family was blessed with the opportunity to own our own home, one of the most exciting aspects of this blessing was that we would not be limited by landlords in our choice of pets. We had been living in a townhouse apartment for a while that did not allow "rug animals." Cats are an essential part of my life and I'd missed the opportunity to share my life with them. Gratefully, my husband and daughter also have this love of feline presence. Shortly before we moved in, we were given the opportunity to share our new home with two beautiful Siamese, Michelle and Pierre. Their previous owner was moving into an apartment and became subject to the limitations on pets we had been forced to endure for two years. Michelle and Pierre were not young cats. We knew that when we agreed to accept their care. Chel was at least eleven and Bear was nearly twelve. Chel was timid and frightened. It took months to win her trust. Bear earned his nickname by loudly proclaiming his needs and dissatisfaction at every opportunity. These animals quickly captured our hearts and our laps. We often wondered what we had done without them. They added so much love to our lives. Every night when Ben and I sat down to rest and "kick back," Chel was on my lap and Bear commanded Ben's. Our lives were full of purr. We felt they'd been a part of us forever. A few months later, Pierre began to grow weak. He had been the biggest, loudest cat I had ever seen, and slowly he dwindled down to skin and bones. It took a while to determine his illness and we watched in agony as he slipped away. When we got the final test results, he had an incurable disease and together, Ben, Joy and I stood in the vet's office, wept, and made the hardest decision of our lives. We had to free Bear of his physical burden. It was an extremely difficult time for our family. Chel suffered the loss of her best friend. My heart was broken. About a week later a friend who didn't know about Bear gave me a gift of a blank journal. She knew I loved to scribble things down. She had left it lying face down on a table. After she'd gone I reached down and picked up the book and as I turned it over, my heart leaped to my throat. Gracing the cover was a beautiful, elegant, alive, Siamese cat that looked exactly like Bear before he got sick. I began to cry. But then I realized in an instant that Pierre was not dead. He was as alive in spirit as I was in the flesh. I got his message loud and clear.

I have often been told to find the child within. Many answers lie with that child, the masters say. That was a difficult concept for me to understand until I had a child of my own to guide to adulthood. Children are – well, children. The innocence, glee, playfulness, and wisdom my daughter was born with are indeed qualities that should be cultivated. Once, when Joy was about six, I was going out of town for a few days and Joy spent the weekend with Ben's parents. We had been separated before, but not too often, and I was never very keen on being separated from the people I loved. I suppose I'm too insecure or possessive. It broke my heart when Joy left for school in the morning or when my husband or I had to go to work. Throughout our brief separation, I missed Joy terribly. My only consolation was hoping she was missing me as much as I missed her. When I got home, I took her in my arms and declared how much I missed her. "Did you miss me too?" I asked her. Joy seemed to think for a minute, and then she replied, "I guess so Mama, but I remembered you."

I believe there are masters, special souls who come to earth, or serve as guides to teach others. They can take many forms and are often personified in a way that makes it difficult for us to recognize them. Many times, we do not, and the opportunity for growth does not occur. A few years ago, I was driving to work one morning in the pouring rain. I'm not a coffee drinker but occasionally I like a soda first thing in the morning. This was one of those occasions. I pulled into the lot of a convenience mart and parked as near to the door as possible. As I was preparing for the dash to the door, I noticed a young man talking on the pay phone outside the building. He was only a few feet in front of my car and he seemed to be staring at me. Oh brother, I thought. I didn't feel like hassling with some creep this morning. He was soaking wet, long hair, dirty jeans – typical creep. I ran to the door, being careful to lock my car and hoped he would be gone when I came out. He wasn't. I could feel his eyes watching me while I unlocked the door and got in. I was relieved. I was safely in my car again without incident. When I looked forward to put the key in the ignition, I caught movement out of the corner of my eye. The man was waving frantically at me. Here we go, I thought. He wasn't making obscene gestures; he was pointing at my car. Still skeptical, I looked directly at him for the first time. He was shouting above the rain, still holding the telephone receiver in his hand. I rolled my window down a hair. He hollered that my right front tire was low. Oh, I thought, okay. I waved a thanks and got out of there. When I was safely at work, I checked my tire.

It was indeed low, almost flat. I sent that young man thoughts of gratitude to try to make up for the multitude of negativity I had sent his way earlier. You never know about people. Sure, it pays to be careful in this time we live in, but on that day, I had been the creep.

I began writing these little stories in honor of my beautiful daughter's eighth birthday in June of 1989. This is some of what that old soul in a tiny body taught me up to that point. It is such a pleasure, a "joy" to be a parent in this enlightened age. It gave my daughter and me an unprecedented opportunity to view each other as equals, on the earth to learn. Neither of us had all the answers, especially Mom. She helped me learn this. I learned that I am not infallible and that she will not love me any less because I admit when I am wrong. When I was wrong and I told her so, she forgave me so easily. I learned that all she expected from me was the truth, always and unconditionally. When I told her the truth; whether about me, about the Universe, about life, the good and the bad, her lovely brown eyes would light up with understanding. I learned, most of all, about love. It is true, when you really love someone, you save the biggest piece of cake for them. The pleasure you receive from watching them eat it far outweighs the pleasure you would have received from the cake. Forgiveness, truth, love. No school, no teacher, no one could have taught me more.

For Valentine's Day when Joy was eight, Ben and I thought it would be really neat to give her a kitten of her very own. She was old enough to accept the responsibility and what better gift of love than an animal, who instinctively loves unconditionally. We searched and searched for the perfect one and finally found a beautiful little blue-eyed Siamese just six weeks old. Joy named him Robin Hood. We lived on Sherwood Avenue. Ben and I called him The Beast. Robin was a very earthy kitten. Unfortunately, he hadn't developed into the higher levels of consciousness yet. Everything belonged to him to do with as he pleased. He did not mind or respond to discipline. He walked on the kitchen table, climbed the curtains, invaded my showers, terrorized our other cats, and leapt to our shoulders with glee and a squeal when we weren't looking. He owned the house. In order to get any sleep at night, we were forced to put all three cats in the basement before retiring. Our family room was downstairs so it wasn't like they were being locked in the cellar. We did have to lock the basement door or Robin opened it and led his band of merry cats back to invade our beds. One morning, after they had been downstairs only a few times, I got up and stumbled to the bathroom, as usual. I opened up the linen closet to grab a towel and I heard scratching coming up from the laundry chute. In a flash, there was Robin, clawing his way out of the hole and into the bathroom at my feet. I opened the bathroom door and he ran for the basement. I assume he felt it his duty to rescue his captured friends. I followed him and opened the basement door. He made a dash for the bottom of the chute. I guess he couldn't believe what he had done any more than I could, so he had to reaffirm his success. There were very few clothes in the laundry chute at the time of his ascent because I had washed the clothes the night before. Robin clawed up a couple of feet of slick boards to get to freedom. After I held the door shut on him the next few mornings, he finally gave up his escape tunnel. But I knew he was planning something. Ben said there was no way we could keep him in the basement against his will. He would always find a way out. Doors are often shut in our faces. Time and time again doors shut and we feel out of control. Friends move away, bills pile up, taxes rise, spouses walk out, or illness hits. The earth plane is sometimes a difficult place to try to live. The saying is that when God shuts a door he opens a window. The window is often difficult to see. When all the windows and doors slam shut, maybe we should try clawing our way up the laundry chute. There is always another way out. There is always an alternative. Perhaps it takes a nine month old earthy terror to show us. I never knew what he was going to do next, but he always found a way to get it done.

Something happened to me that offered proof of how connected the events in our lives really are and it helps me remember that anything is possible. When I first started studying philosophy and spirituality, everything was new and exciting to me. Previously, I had only been exposed to the religion I grew up with and I remember reading for the first time about the balance of male and female principles in the world. I had never been exposed to the concept of the feminine side of the Universe. I was taught God was male. That was it. I was also taught females were born inferior to males. It was just the way things were. I never liked the concept, even as a little girl, but had become more or less resigned to it. So imagine my excitement when I began to learn that there were other viewpoints! One book I read suggested getting a feminine image to keep in my home as a reminder of the "power of the feminine." I thought that was a good idea but had no clue where to find such a thing. After thinking about it for a while, I remembered a little plastic statue of Mary I'd had as a child. My aunt from Texas had given it to me. My mother's oldest sister never married, started teaching school as a teenager, put herself through college in the early 1900s, became a missionary, and after earning her doctorate, eventually a college professor. She was an enigma to me. Every summer she came home and visited her brothers and sisters and their families, spending a week at a time with each. My father hated those visits and he didn't seem to like her being around much. We weren't exactly close as she had dozens of nieces and nephews, but I always looked forward to her being around and she gave such interesting presents. One time she gave me this little statue. I don't know why she even had it. She wasn't Catholic and it was an odd thing for her to have. I kept it on my dresser at my parents' house for years. I even marked it once with red fingernail polish when I was a bit careless doing my nails. Like all young people, when I left home I left some things behind. Mother eventually boxed it up, and put it in a closet for a while and then threw most of it out. It was nothing I really wanted, old toys and papers, but I remembered that my little statue had been among that stuff. I thought it would be a perfect reminder of the balance I was searching for. I went to Mother's and began to hunt. By that time, I'd been away from home nearly ten years and my stuff was mostly gone. So was my statue. End of story, I thought. About five years later, I was at a rummage sale. I was walking up and down the aisles of tables and looking at all the junk. I spotted a statue just like the one I'd lost! I was surprised, then puzzled when I picked it up and there on the front was the familiar little dab of red nail polish. It wasn't like the one I lost. It was the one I lost! How in the world did it get there, miles from my home town and years from when I last saw it? I inquired but no one knew who had donated it. So, of course, I bought it and brought it home. It is a perfect reminder, but not only of feminine energy. Every time I look at it, I see unity and balance and cycles of life way beyond my understanding. I see my aunt and all that she achieved against the odds. Anything is possible.

How many times do we make decisions based on what we think we know or want and ignore what the Universe may have to offer us? I wonder what we miss by our predetermined ideas of how something should look or be. Sometimes we take no notice of what may be right under our noses. As I ponder this question, I am reminded of how our kitty friend, Ariel came into our lives. When we adopted her, we already had an elderly Siamese female, Chel and Robin Hood was a mischievous kitten, so I thought we should look for another breed, just to add some variety to the mix. I saw in the paper that our local animal rescue had Manx kittens. Ben and I went to take a look. There were six of them, all black with varying degrees of white splotches. Three had tails and three did not, which I learned is typical of a

Manx litter. I've never seen a kitten I didn't immediately love and this group was adorable. As I was playing with them, their caregiver asked if I'd like to see the mother, to know what they might be like as adults. She brought her out and told us her sad story of abandonment. She was young, less than a year, but fully grown. Not at all what I was looking for. I kept playing with the kittens, trying to decide which of the tailless ones I wanted to adopt, barely noticing the mom cat. She shyly came over to me and began to wrap around my legs and mew quietly. I kept my attention on the kittens. It was a big decision. The mother cat would not stop rubbing against me until finally I looked her square in the eyes. I said, "Ben, I think we need to take this one." He was surprised and asked if I was sure. I looked at the kittens one more time, but by now the mother cat was practically in my lap. She had chosen me. I wouldn't trade the sixteen years of gentle companionship she shared with us for any kitten in the world. I often marvel at how close I came to choosing someone else – just because I had already made up my mind that we wanted a kitten, or so I thought. With every decision we make, we should look beyond that decision to what else might be curling in our laps.

New Year's has always been a curious holiday for me. It marks the end of an exhausting holiday season and the beginning of a couple of very cold months, and yet, for most people, it is a time of anticipation for the future. People dress up and go out or party with friends and family, anxiously waiting the turn of the clock to midnight and the start of a whole New Year. Years ago, someone told me that the way you presented yourself at midnight marked the kind of year that you would have. In theory, if we dress up and have a really good time, our year will be prosperous and happy. But what happens the next morning? We start the year out tired, or worse, hung over. For many people, the first new day of the year is spent recuperating and recovering from the night before. I like a party as much as the next person, and I have been to some really great New Year's bashes. I'm not advocating we give those up. But maybe, no matter where we are at midnight on New Year's Eve, the secret isn't about what we're wearing or what we're doing or even who we're with. Maybe if we just grab the feeling of positive anticipation, it would be enough. We can do that anywhere, even dressed in our comfy pajamas, all by ourselves!

I've written so much about my cats. I've written about Pierre, the Bear and all the lessons my family learned through his departure from this life. I've written about J.C., the former Siamese love of my life, who has been gone for years. I've written about Robin (the Beast) Hood, Joy's cat and our constant source of material about life's challenges. And I've written about Ariel, our fairy cat. All of these cats were so special, so unique, each in their own way. I have not yet written about Michelle. Chel lived with us and shared our home just like the other cats. I've allowed myself to feel a little guilty because I've not found anything unique to write about Chel. Let's face it, she was a boring cat. She was old when we got her. She was slightly overweight and occasionally her fur came out in patches on her back because of a skin condition. She had a tremble and her Siamese eyes were faded blue. But, we loved her so much that I decided to write about our Chel anyway. Chel didn't do anything. She never played like the younger cats. She never got into anything or caused a scene. In fact, the only annoying thing she ever did was constantly demand to sit on our laps. Every time one of us sat down, Chel would come running as fast as her little old legs could go and jump up into our laps. It was a real bother when we sat down to tie a shoe. She was insistent and quickly curled up and made herself at home. We hated to make her get down because she purred so. She was so satisfied just being near us. That's all she asked of us. I guess it is a pretty boring existence to just live to give and receive love. There really isn't anything she can teach us. But I'm glad I finally wrote about her anyway.

Several years ago I was called to serve on a jury. I learned a lot through this experience. At first, I thought I would try to get out of serving, as many people do, but once I was at the courtroom, my civic mindedness and desire for justice kicked in and I became a willing participant. Real trials aren't like the ones we see on TV, but there is still a great deal of drama. I was fascinated by the production. The first thing that stood out to me was the way I was treated as a juror. The bailiff saw to our every need. People were always checking to see if we were okay, even the judge. Everyone in the courtroom stood up as we entered and left the room. The jurors make decisions that will affect many lives for years to come. Our judgment, opinions and experience was respected. No one asked us to prove ourselves. We were respected as human beings and treated as such. Often in our day to day life, this isn't the case. After one day out in the world, you can begin to feel as if there is no courtesy or respect left. It was refreshing to be treated as a worthwhile person. How wonderful the world would be if we only valued each other just a little more. Perhaps many people don't deserve our respect, but most do. I'm not for bringing back the age of chivalry when men stood up when a woman entered a room, but I think in our hearts we should stand up for all human kind just because we're all so wonderfully human and try to respect each other more often. It certainly feels good.

We knew nothing about the Manx cat when we brought Ariel home but she quickly taught us what we needed to know. The Manx has long, strong back legs and hops just like a rabbit. Our new roommate had no tail, just a bit of fluff. We laughed and laughed at her peculiar movements. She was barely grown, still very playful, but shy. Her darting amber eyes, big and round, expressed her mistrust of humans and the hurt she had been through. Her fur was black but dotted with white hairs, much like snowflake obsidian. We couldn't catch or hold her because she didn't trust us. She reminded us of an elusive fairy and so we named her Ariel. At night, while we were asleep or when we were gone from the house, she pulled books out of the shelves and into the floor. These weren't just any books, but ones it seems she thought we needed to read. The books were always metaphysical or inspirational or had a connection with something going on in our lives. Ben, Joy and I are all book collectors, so Ariel had a large selection to choose from. Ariel was a delight. She was one of the sweetest natured cats I'd ever known. She sang and trilled when she purred. She would gently play with anything and everything, batting softly at the phone cord or hopping after a wisp of dust on the floor. For a while, Ben and I heard Ariel lunging at the bedroom walls at night after we were in bed. I assumed she was chasing fairies that only she could see, but Ben made a discovery that proved me wrong. Ariel sat hour after hour and stared at one or the other walls on either side of the bed. If I was downstairs in the family room watching TV at night and came upstairs once or twice in a three hour period, Ariel would have never moved. She sat in the dark, night after night. One morning, Ben told me that he'd finally figured out what Ariel was doing every night. Whenever we pulled the shade down over the window in the bedroom, there was a little crack on either side. Every time a car passed down our street, its headlights shone – just for a second – on one of the bedroom walls. Ariel sat hour after hour waiting for the light. She knew it would come. It always did. She waited patiently for just a glimpse. She jumped at it, but always missed. And then, the light was gone. Ariel was never discouraged. She'd seen it, reached for it and she had faith that it would come again; no matter how much darkness was in between. Someday, if she waited long enough, and kept trying to reach it, that light would be hers.

All the time I was growing up, my mother was a real promoter of music. My sisters and I took piano lessons, sang in the church choir and played in the school band. My father seemed only to tolerate our practicing, barely at times. He didn't even sing in church. He just held the hymnbook. I always thought he was musically challenged. When I was a teenager I begged for and finally got a guitar. I tried to teach myself to play and my cousin was engaged for a few lessons, but finally I gave up. There just wasn't anyone to teach me. Years later, after Dad retired and my mother was ill, imagine my surprise when my sister mentioned that Dad had bought a guitar. I couldn't believe it. An even bigger shock came the next time I visited him. He put on an

LP, and played and sang along! I thought I had slipped into another dimension. He must have noticed my astonishment because he pulled me aside and told me a story. When he was a sophomore in high school, he and two other boys performed a musical comedy skit during a school talent show. They played and sang like "hillbillies" and dressed the part. They didn't win but the crowd roared and they had a ball. On the way home from school that day Dad's older brother who was a junior at the same school, jumped him and beat him up. He told Dad he was embarrassed by his behavior and never to do that again. Dad never did. He put away his guitar and never again let anyone see him "perform," for nearly sixty years that is. It was only when the circumstances of his life changed with Mother's illness, that he could let go of the fear of what others thought and find his music again. The last years of his life, he played and sang every day. I have that guitar. I wouldn't trade it for anything.

We found out not long after Pierre died that he had feline infectious peritonitis. It is a disease which can lay dormant for many years and is very contagious among cats. Some cats carry it but never develop the symptoms. Since we had Pierre a very short time, we had no idea how long he'd had the disease or where he had contracted it. We also did not know if his partner, Michelle carried the disease or if our baby cat, Robin had brought it into the household. Robin could have been healthy when we brought him home and was now at risk. The big question: Do we have Michelle and Robin tested, a long and inconclusive process? If we bring another cat into our home, are we inflicting a death sentence on him or her? Joy, Ben and I discussed the situation for many agonizing hours. We prayed for an answer. We felt we could not live in a world without cats. We decided that Michelle and Robin were family, for better or worse. Knowing that they carried a time-bomb would not alter our love for them. We decided not to have them tested. We took what precautions we could, replacing food dishes and litter box, and welcomed Ariel into our home. Still, we were very much aware that Pierre's fate could, at any time, take another of our precious purr balls. Every time Chel sneezed or Robin slept in, I prayed that we would not be put through losing another friend. We decided not to enlarge our cat family again, while the danger was still present in the cats that lived with Pierre. That meant no more cats as long as Chel, Robin and Ariel were alive. Robin and Ariel were both less than two years old so it was a long sentence. When Pierre died, our vet sent a donation in his honor to a research facility at Purdue University. They work to find cures and vaccines for the incurable diseases which plague our animal friends. We were very gratified to know that she did that. Almost a year after Bear died we received a pamphlet from the vet. The research scientists at Purdue had made a breakthrough. A vaccine was now available for feline infectious peritonitis. We had all our precious friends vaccinated. The death sentence had been lifted from our home. My prayers didn't save Pierre. But his death contributed to a vaccine that would save countless other cats, including our own. Sometimes prayers are answered.

I always marvel at those people who come right out of school knowing exactly what they will do with the rest of their lives. Of course, in today's world there is such uncertainty in the job market. Just ask any nightly news reporter. I saw one report recently that declared graduates would be having a tougher time than ever finding the jobs they want in their fields. I guess that is true, but I wonder how many people who plan out their lives ever get to actually do what they expect? I think the very nature of life is uncertainty, no matter what is going on with the economy or the world in general. If we stick too closely to a plan, there is much we might miss. Not to mention how frustrated we get when something unexpected happens. How do you plan for life's ups and downs? I don't think you do. It's okay to have goals – necessary in fact – but a bit of flexibility is essential in dealing with life. The truth is, we just don't know what might happen on any given day. If we wake up every morning with the thought that we are looking forward to the possibilities and accept the twists and turns life throws at us we may be better off than anything we could have possibly imagined. I have never known anyone who claims to have lived their lives exactly as they planned. There are just too many variables. And yet, we all fight so hard to maintain control. Gee. I wonder what we've all missed.

Have you ever known someone who personifies Universal Love? I doubt it. As humans, we aspire toward that goal, but it is only an aspiration. Miss Chel lived to love, to give it and receive it. She personified love, even though she was not a person. Perhaps we need to remove ourselves from our personhood in order to live lives of love. It is the needs of the personality that keep us from this lofty goal, yet it is our personality that makes each of us uniquely a person, with the endless capacity for love. What, then, is the answer? I think it is to aspire to leave this life as our beloved friend did, purring, in the arms of someone who loved her.

The bravest cat I ever knew was our dear friend Rosebud. Rosie has been gone a long time now and she only lived for eight short years but she had a lot to teach us. After Pierre and Michelle died, we decided to add to our family once again. She came from a humane society shelter. We were looking through the room with all the cages and I noticed that Ben had stopped in his tracks. When I went back to him, he said this one is it. I looked at the cat in the cage. She was a beautiful tri-colored gray, tan and cream with big amber eyes. The tone in Ben's voice told me not to question this choice. Something in him was very sure. They had bonded instantly. We brought her home and were not disappointed. She was an affectionate one year old who fit into our family instantly. I can still see her lying under the Christmas tree every year and dancing around the kitchen, begging for treats, which she always got. When Rosie started getting sick, I didn't expect anything too dire, but when the tests came back, she tested positive for diabetes. At first we gave her pills everyday, not an easy thing, but manageable.

Soon though, the disease progressed until we were up to two shots a day. I never dreamed I could give a shot to anyone but all of us learned how, even Joy, so that Rosebud would always be taken care of on time. You would have never known she was sick. She went about her life with an attitude of gratefulness that amazed us all. Whenever Rosie lay down on something, she would always scoot to the edge and hang her head over the side. It was her trademark stance. We used to laugh and say she was getting a new perspective that way. Maybe she was. She had been abandoned and discarded early in her life. Now she was very ill. From her perspective, she was with a family that loved her and took care of her. From that point of view, nothing else mattered. Maybe perspective is all that matters.

All mothers know one of their responsibilities is to be "on call" all the time, whenever their child has a question or concern. It is not always easy to talk to children. They usually come up with things at times when we are the least prepared. Five minutes before bed, Joy would ask me about some complicated aspect of adult lives – like sex. One of the neat things about raising my daughter was that I always tried to tell her the truth about things and she has always known that the world is not perfect, but for a reason. She accepts this. At one of those rare times when I started a question/answer period with her, I learned much more than Joy. She was probably about nine years old and I noticed that something seemed to be bothering her. I was quizzing her to try to get her to open up. I reassured her that she could ask me anything, knowing full well she might do just that. Finally, she said she did have a question. I was momentarily relieved. Now I would get a clue as to what was troubling her. "Mama?" she asked, "why are we here on the earth?" I was disappointed. She had made up a question instead of opening up, I thought. I went into my usual explanation for the hundredth time. This was one of her favorite questions. I told her about the earth being a school where we have the opportunity to learn lessons. And with each lesson we learn we grow spiritually. "You know what I think, Mama?" she interrupted me right in the middle of my spiel. I gave her the floor. "I think we are each given a ladder. Some of our ladders are longer than others. Each wrung of the ladder is a life. When we get to the top, we get to be with God. See, God used to be real big but when we all broke off, God got real small. As each one of us gets to the top of our ladders, God will start getting big until we are all there together and God will be real big again." I was speechless. My mind took Joy's explanation and ran with it. It was so simple and yet so true. I asked her where she heard this information but she just shrugged and looked at the ceiling. It doesn't matter where Joy learned this little philosophy of hers but that at age nine she could espouse it, believe it, and share it! It was so incredible. She was light years away from where I was at her age. I was so grateful.

Cats, of course, are not the only animals we can learn from. I believe every one, every thing we come in contact with while we are on the earth serves as our teachers. We only have to be open to learn. Years ago, a friend told me a delightful story of a lesson she had learned from her dog. Her husband had died a few years before, after many years of marriage. She was sharing her home with her beloved friend, a terrier named Dan. Dan usually slept at the foot of her bed, but one night she awoke to loud snoring on the other pillow next to her head. She hadn't had that experience since her husband's departure from the earth, but she responded from an old habit and reached over in the dark and sleepily poked her dozing dog. The snoring quit and she turned over to settle back into sleep. No sooner had she drifted off than the snoring began again. She reached over to poke again, but stopped herself in mid-poke. By this time, she was awake enough to realize that Dan's snoring no longer seemed an annoyance, but a blessed reminder that she was not alone.

I have often said that our teachers come in many unusual packages. I wonder why I am still surprised when I learn a lesson from an animal or a child, the best teachers of all. The child of a friend of mine brought me a little weed and urged me to eat it. I trusted his knowledge of wild food completely. His mom was an herbalist and constantly taught him about the natural world. He had learned more in his eleven years than I ever will. I popped the little seed pods into my mouth. Wow! It was a spicy little thing, similar to a very hot radish straight from the garden. With my mouth still burning, I said, "How could you?" He just grinned and continued munching on his shepherd's purse. He liked the spicy little weed. I learned it was one of his favorite treats. I teased him the rest of the day and vowed to get even with him for giving me a burning mouth. I was grateful that I didn't suffer any after affects. A few days later out of curiosity, I looked up the shepherd's purse in an herb dictionary. I had been asking for healing for certain ailments, annoyances really, for several months. I read that the little weed my friend had given me was used to treat several of my complaints. I was stunned. Was it just a coincidence? Did he somehow sense that I would benefit from his favorite treat? We ask and ask for healing. I wonder how many times the Universe gives us answers and we never hear? I guess he taught me more than one lesson that day.

SECTION FIVE

Make sure your subconscious knows you love it by stroking it until it purrs.

Ben was on his way to work very early one rainy Tuesday morning. He had just crossed the Ohio River bridge and was coming up to the place where the road splits into two interstates. He looked up and suddenly in front of him was a very slow moving garbage truck. The truck had no lights to indicate that it was moving slowly so Ben had no warning. It was just there. He slammed on his breaks and his truck spun over to the side of the road barely missing the guardrail. It kept spinning back across the highway and he ended up facing the wrong way in the V-shaped medium at the split. The garbage truck just kept moseying along and got off at the next exit. As Ben sat there composing himself, he realized that there were no other cars around. He also realized that if there had been, he would have hit them all. When he told me about this later that day, we both were just very thankful that he was okay and his truck was okay and that there had not really been an accident. I think our focus was so much on what hadn't happened and what could have happened that we didn't consider why this had happened – other than the slow moving garbage truck. The very next week Ben was again on his way to work. As he left our house and stopped at the first stop sign on our street, something he has done thousands of times, he saw another car stop to his right. Somehow, he and the other car ended up moving forward at the same time and Ben hit the other car. He doesn't know how it happened but the police officer thought that they both assumed the other vehicle was stopped. It really wasn't anybody's fault.

I think it is too much of a "coincidence" after years of not having an accident, Ben had these two experiences so close together. The first incident ended without an actual accident, but it could have been very serious. The second incident ended with an actual accident but very little damage to either vehicle and no one was hurt. I think that if something is "supposed" to happen, it happens. I think Ben was supposed to have an accident. He didn't have to endure a serious one. Why was he supposed to have an accident? He's the only one who can figure that out (I'm not about to interpret his "signs"), but I do believe that all of us need to be paying closer attention to everything, all the time.

When Ariel was around 15, our vet found a rather large tumor in her abdomen. The surgery discovered the tumor had attached to her spleen and both were removed. The vet was certain that the tumor was malignant. We asked for help sending healing to Ariel from everyone we knew. When the report came back from the lab, to the shock of our vet, the tumor was "totally benign." Not only that, but Ariel's incision healed up perfectly, even though Ariel had pulled out all of her stitches only two days after surgery. Ben made a mad dash to meet our vet (bless her) on a Sunday night. Everyone at the vet's office was amazed at how well she healed. I'm not. I know the power of healing prayer. One other thing makes this story successful. Being a cat, Ariel had no resistance to the healing. She didn't worry about it. She didn't know the odds or possibilities. She was just an open, willing subject that let our healing through. That's harder for us to do with our "advanced" awareness and intelligence. Next time you are ill, you might take a lesson from our Ariel and cat-like, just be open and receptive to the healing that surrounds you always. Don't think about it, don't question it and never believe it when a medical person tells you they are certain about your condition. Nothing is certain except that healing energy is always there for you.

I stopped taking Tae Kwon Do classes in the early 1980s. I never imagined that I would eventually resume my study and achieve a black belt. Ben and I were just looking for an exercise activity we could do together when the opportunity arose for us to check out a Tae Kwon Do school. I was so nervous that first day we went. Everyone there was younger, stronger and more fit than me. I adopted the attitude that I was just there for the exercise and didn't care what anyone else thought and I certainly didn't think about testing for belts. As I watched other students test and pass through the belt levels I decided that I could do the first test and earn a yellow belt. Tae Kwon Do is set up so that each belt level only focuses on the requirements for that level. You are not allowed to practice above your level. At each step along the way I had the same realization. Step by step, we advanced through the nine levels to black belt. I'm not suggesting it was easy. There were many times I thought about giving up. But as long as I stayed focused on where I was and didn't look too far ahead I was able to stay with it. I think that is true of everything in life. We usually give up when the goal is so huge in our minds that we can't even take the step by step process to get there. Maybe we shouldn't think of the goal at all but only the first step – and then the next.

A few years ago, a horse won the Kentucky Derby that no one expected. This happens now and again in horse racing, I'm told, but the opportunities to see the Universe at work are just astounding when you look at the win that shouldn't have been. I'm talking about Giacomo, the horse that didn't have a prayer to win the Kentucky Derby in 2005, but did. Here's what occurred to me after hearing all the reports and speculations about how this thing could have happened. As long as you don't know you are supposed to lose, you can win. Sometimes you have a guide (or jockey) that puts you in just the right place at the right time to maneuver through whatever is blocking your way. Sometimes "the field" slows down for whatever reason. Sometimes others get too cocky and sure of themselves and try to win too big. They spread themselves thin and don't accomplish a thing. Sometimes breeding far in the past shines through and unknown talent is displayed. Some days are just lucky. The point is, as long as you keep trying to do the thing you want to do – run your heart out – someday all the factors may come together in your favor and you will win in spite of the odds. Of course, there is the possibility that day won't come, like it didn't for nineteen other horses. But don't you want to be there – in the race – just in case it does?

When Ben and I started back into Tae Kwon Do, the founder and grandmaster of the school we joined was very ill. He passed away and we were never able to meet him. Besides being very accomplished at Tae Kwon Do, he was also a very wise and personable man. We have learned about him through the stories of his students, who are now our teachers. When we told our instructor that we were going on vacation, he said that Grandmaster always said everyone should take a vacation at least once a year, because of what you learn on a vacation. I pondered that, and it occurred to me that this was very good advice. If we stay rooted in our routines, we learn very little. It is a safe place to be and sometimes we need that safety but I think we should push ourselves to explore beyond what we feel is our safety zone. Vacations force us to do that because we are in a new place, dealing with different issues and away from our proverbial safety blankets. I always come back from vacation with an appreciation of home, an inspiration to look at my work with refreshed eyes, and I always learn about myself as I experience different situations. This is, of course, beyond the obvious education I get about new places, people, and situations. If you feel you can't afford a vacation or if you feel you can't take time away, try to take at least a "vacation day" as often as possible. Take a day off from your routine; explore something you would not normally do, as if you were on vacation. Give yourself every opportunity to learn.

Ben and I made a trip to Chicago a few years ago to visit the museums. It had been years since either of us had been there and I didn't ever recall driving in downtown Chicago. All went well until we exited to Lake Shore Drive. There was a lot of construction around and somehow we ended up going the wrong way. It got me thinking about how often in life we end up going the wrong way. Sometimes we just get carried along with the flow of the "traffic" and don't even realize for a while that we aren't headed in the direction we meant to be going. After all, everything in the future looks unfamiliar. Sometimes, as happened to us, it is hard to find a place to turn around and head back the right way. It is a hassle and so we often just keep moving along, even when we figure out we're going the wrong way. We can end up in an undesirable "neighborhood" that way. It can be so annoying after a long trip to realize that you have to turn around and do the last however many miles over. It is time consuming and tiring and takes a lot of effort. But if we decide not to turn around, not to do it over, we never get where we wanted to go. How much sense does that make?

A few years ago, on the 4th of July, Ben and I walked with our Tae Kwon Do school in a parade. We'd done this before, but that year we were positioned right in front of the high school marching band. As we started walking down the street, I could clearly hear the cadence from the snare drums and the band striking up their school song. Something happened to me. My whole body responded as if I were one of those high school marchers. My knees came up and I marched in step. I whirled my head around to see if my line was straight. My fingers wrapped around my "saxophone" and moved with the notes of "On Wisconsin." Wow! It had been years since I marched with my high school band. We were so disciplined and drilled back then. Our director was determined to have a winning marching band, and we were. I've always enjoyed watching marching bands since then but this was the first time I'd ever been plopped right in the midst of one. Whatever is drilled into us, whatever makes an impression on our subconscious mind, whatever experience is remembered can resurface at any time and we will respond as we did when the event was programmed, unless we see it for what it is: a past memory, not a current reality. We can choose how to respond if we are aware of what is happening. Luckily, on that 4th, I was able to easily see where my response was coming from and resisted the urge to run back into the band, grab a sax and join in!

For some reason, vampires seem to be very popular characters these days. My favorite vampire was a character on the series "Buffy the Vampire Slayer." His name was Spike and when he showed up in the second season of the show, he was rightly called, "The Big Bad." He had been a vampire for over 300 years and had cut a path of destruction that was unrivaled in history. He had killed many innocent people and done, in his words, "unspeakable" things, and enjoyed it. In the Buffy mythology, vampires are made by other vampires (it's a blood-sucking thing) and when the process is complete, the humanity, the soul of the individual is gone, but many of their personality traits remain intact. Spike, in life had been a weak man named William who wrote bad poetry about a girl he could never have and was dominated by his ailing mother. He was beset with unrequited love. His obsession with love remained with him in his monster state and became the undoing of the fiend within him. He fell in love with the Vampire Slayer. As the seasons rolled on, Spike found himself unable to deny his love for Buffy which eventually turned him from a fiend into a hero. By the end of the series he had gone to great lengths to have his soul returned to him and in the very last episode, sacrificed himself to save the world for the woman he loved. What I found most interesting is throughout Spike's transition, everyone around him continued to distrust him and think of him as a monster no matter what good he did. Over and over again, he had to calmly tell them that he was, after all, a vampire and only did what vampires do. He was good now and he had changed. No apologies, no excuses. He was what he was and now he was different. You know, I think that is the key to erasing guilt from our lives. Whatever we did, said, or didn't do or didn't say, it is always in the past. It is who we were then. That no longer matters. What matters is who we are now, in the present. We are never who we were. We are always changing. What happened in the past was done by someone else. True, we aren't vampires – at least most of us aren't – and haven't done the kinds of things monsters do, but we have done the kinds of things humans do.

A new job requires making major adjustments in our lives. When Ben changed jobs it was somewhat challenging, as any change is. His hours fluctuated every day and all or our routines were disturbed. We adjusted and adapted. Not so with our kitty friends. It became apparent to me, as we lived through hours of Siamese elocution, that Robin Hood did not adjust well at all. Even Miss Ariel, who rarely speaks, got mouthy and restless. I was listening to the meow chorus one morning as Ben was desperately trying to sleep and I realized why it was so hard for them and why it is so hard for us to manifest change in our lives. Our subconscious is like our animal friends. It knows what is supposed to happen based on what has always happened before. If it does not get what it wants, it "screams" until it gets its way. It may even make us sick! There is no way to tell it through our conscious minds that a change needs to take place. I begged the cats to please be quiet so "Daddy" could sleep. They just looked at me and continued their tirade. They couldn't understand. They wouldn't understand until enough time of the new routine replaced the memory of the old. Until then, we had to endure their discomfort. When we try to manifest change in our lives, we often give up too soon, long before our subconscious has accepted the new way of thinking. It takes time to manifest change. In the meantime, do what I did with Robin and Ariel: make sure your subconscious knows you love it by stroking it until it purrs and remember to play with it every day.

A few years ago, a group of us went to Indianapolis to hear a lecture by a well known author. I was fortunate enough to be chosen to ask her a question. In her books she refers to each of us having life themes. I asked her what my themes were. She said justice and winning. I have pondered this ever since, trying to make it fit into my life. Just the other day a memory came back to me from high school. I played alto saxophone in the band, and all through high school I wanted to be first chair. We would try out every six weeks and that position always went to an upperclassman. When I was a senior, I thought my time had come. But the first chair position went to another girl in my class. I was very unhappy about this because I knew I had outplayed her. She was a popular girl. Our band director had his favorites and those people usually got selected for the first chair positions. I remember feeling that it was totally unfair – unjust. For a while, I stewed about it but then I had an idea. If I worked really hard and really showed her up, he could not overlook me again. It worked. I practiced and practiced and played my tryout piece perfectly. He had to give me the chair. We often think of justice as something that should just be part of the balance of the universe. I don't think it necessarily is. If we want justice in our lives, we have to work for it. Sometimes by winning, we can balance the universe ourselves.

When she was younger, our beautiful kitty friend, Ariel used to do this very special thing that made us laugh and endeared her totally to our hearts. Being a Manx, she was somewhat less graceful than other cats. She had only a stump of a tail so her balance was not perfect. Her back legs and hind quarters were shaped more like a rabbit than a cat. She had large back feet that could hop across a room faster than most cats could run. If she found a tiny piece of lint or paper on the floor, she would elegantly rise up on those big back feet as if she were on her toes and delicately bat that paper with her right front paw while holding her left paw out for balance. We called it her ballet. It had to be a small piece of paper because Miss Ariel was very shy and anything very big frightened her. After the first performance, we often tore up little pieces of paper for further shows. As she got older she danced less frequently. She still loved to play but mostly by lying on the bed, while I ran around and chased the toys she batted. I honestly don't remember the last time we saw her dance, until...

Ariel was not herself. We were worried sick. Countless trips to the vet. Try this, try that. Pills. Shots. She was so strong and brave. For an elderly kitty, she was still doing a lot of the things she always did. She had the loudest purr. She loved sitting on our laps. But we knew. And then, one day Ben and I were working in the office, sitting on either side of the desk. The closet door was open because that is where we keep our files. We heard a sound and looked toward the closet. There was Miss Ariel dancing her way out of the closet with a little piece of paper that she'd found. We both gasped and then cried. The dance lasted only seconds. For just a few seconds she was a kitten again. In those few seconds she took us back through all the years, sixteen of them, we had shared with her. At first I thought, oh, she must be feeling better; she's doing her ballet! And then I realized she wasn't playing with a tiny piece of paper. She was giving us a gift, a gift that I will cherish forever. When I think of her now I don't see the illness that took her. I see one last ballet.

 I admit it. I am hooked on talent competition reality shows. I think it goes back to being raised on "Ted Mack's Amateur Hour" or perhaps because my mother entered me in every talent show throughout my childhood. Yes, I won one when I was eight but that's another story. My sister in Florida and I email back and forth about every contestant and the show. It's fun to discuss the ups and downs and guess who is going to be voted off. One of the guest mentors on a show we watch was the sixties singer, Lulu. She was terrific on the show and my sister and I discussed her at length. My sister mentioned that Lulu had once been married to "someone" but she couldn't remember who. I had no idea. It drove her crazy trying to remember but I pretty much shrugged it off. About a week later Ben and I were playing a round of Trivial Pursuit. One of the questions on my card was, "Who was Lulu married to?" You know, no matter how "trivial," every question we put out into the Universe is answered. It has happened to me too many times to be a coincidence. I think when the question is big or important we sometimes ignore the answer when it comes, or perhaps we ignore it because we don't agree with the answer. But it always comes. All we have to do is pay attention. And by the way, it was Maurice Gibb.

Everyone worries about the quality of Christmas. They are afraid the economy or other unforeseen circumstances will put a damper on the festivities. You know what I remember as the best holiday memories from the past? Every year as a child I practiced with the church choir for weeks. The Sunday before Christmas, we performed our cantata. The chills and beauty of unpolished voices raised in the harmony of beautiful music. I remember the smell of the sack of oranges, apples and peanuts that were our treat after we performed. I remember gatherings of friends over the years, the faces have changed, but the coming together remains one of the true joys of the holiday season. I think about my first tree after I left my parents' home. No money. No tinsel. Just two college students, some construction paper and lots of popcorn and laughter. I remember my daughter being discharged from the hospital on Christmas Day when she was eight years old after nearly dying from a ruptured appendix. No Christmas dinner that year. Oh, how we didn't mind. I think about a particularly difficult holiday meal with my family and coming home to find that Ben had cleaned the apartment from top to bottom and fixed a huge bowl of fresh strawberries, my favorite. So honestly, I don't think the economy enters into my holiday spirit at all. I don't remember the gifts I've received over the years or the ones bought for others. I just know that every day is filled with blessings and why should the holiday season be any different?

A Valentine for Andrew (1980-2006) Written February 2007

Poet, artist, writer, rapper, singer, dancer, guitarist, musical technician, computer genius, philosopher, militant, student, cook, vegan, connoisseur, friend, lover, son, cousin, nephew, grandson, brother, employee, arguer, debater, confidant, talker, Scorpio, political activist, nurturer, healer, animal lover, rebel...all of these things and more were the mantle you wore. But I know who you really were and are. Before I knew you, while I knew you and especially now, you are Spirit. Just as I am. Just as all of us are – joined together as One Force of Life. If I ever doubted it, and of course, I have, I have you to thank for making it obvious to me that our true nature lasts forever. You have helped us so much the last three months. You have guided us to just what we needed to see, find, hear, and know about you. We feel you and hear you and know you are here. You have comforted us, led us, and inspired us more than I would have ever believed. And I thought myself a believer. We miss the mantle that you were during your brief stay on this Earth. But just as we are supposed to do, we will learn from you forever.

I could write volumes about what I have learned from animal friends who have shared my life. It is true that they can't talk to me or give me advice but just in the act of caring for them and observing them the lessons abound. For example, in December 2007, Robin Hood turned seventeen. The year before when Ariel died, Robin became our last and only animal in residence. This was because he would not tolerate others sharing his abode, except for me and Ben, of course. We decided that due to his advanced age and exalted state, for the rest of his life we would give him anything he wanted, any time, anywhere. We've always "spoiled" our animal friends but never to the degree that Robin enjoyed. When he'd meow, and he did often being a Siamese talker, I dropped everything and tended to his wants. I never put him off or ignored his pleas. I never put myself before his requests. A curious thing happened during this process. The more of my time and energy I gave to Robin the better it made me feel. I found myself more attentive to the needs of others as well. So many times we are too busy or too tired or too something to pay attention to someone else. It's true, not everyone is an aged and wise feline with big blue eyes, and sometimes people take advantage of us, but most of the time what you give to others comes back to you ten-fold.

Some people believe that the purpose of humanity's existence on this planet is to learn integration. That means we have to accept everyone on the planet as part of ourselves and embrace our differences. There is no doubt we still have a long way to go in this world where bigotry and fear seem to have a healthy hold on so many. But there are signs that progress is being made and I am encouraged. One of the most gratifying signs of all happened during the 2008 presidential election. Put politics aside for a moment and consider the top four candidates. The Mormon people were practically chased into the Pacific Ocean in our society's attempt to rid itself of their presence. Blacks have been subjected to centuries of physical and psychological torture. There was no more wrongly maligned group than the young men returning home from Vietnam. Women didn't even have the right to vote when my own mother was born. These four serious candidates for the presidency would not have been taken seriously or even allowed to run for office just a short time ago. True, these signs can be invalidated if we look at the world as a whole where injustice for groups can easily be found. Our country is viewed as a world leader and if the majority of our population of people can appreciate the value of individuals without regard to race, gender, religion or stigma then it will have an impact worldwide. We've never done it before. The importance of these events was staggering. For a moment, stand in awe with me.

SECTION SIX

Love stays in your heart forever.

I've never been one to pay a lot of attention to age and getting older. I know, for some people each birthday that passes marks a scary point of no return. As I contemplated my birthday yet again a few years ago, I was reminded by the presence of my aged and wise kitty friend that it is no big deal. Robin Hood was old by cat standards. That was his nineteenth year. The thing was, he didn't know that. Yes, certain things were different for him. He was a champion jumper and climber in his youth but now his legs did not react for him as they once did. He didn't know that, either. Ben and I were beside ourselves, making our home "older cat friendly." We added steps to the bed and took down his climbing tree. We moved furniture around so that it would be easier for him to sleep where he chose. We lifted him up and down from the couch. You see, Robin would jump just as he always had done, only now he had a tendency to fall. He never once thought he was too old to do anything he decided might be fun. He still ran through the house and up and down the stairs screaming with glee. We tried to tell him to act his age before he hurt himself, but he just ignored us. I wonder what we would do if we didn't know how old we were? I wonder how we would act? What we might accomplish? Maybe we would "fall" sometimes, but I bet just like Robin our purr would be as loud as ever.

The holiday season arrives every December. But in 2009, in my household, there was an event that may have been even more important. Our beautiful Capricorn cat (on the cusp of Sagittarius), Robin Hood had a birthday. He was twenty years old! Twenty years before, our daughter Joy was eight years old. On December 18th of that year her appendix ruptured. It was all bad. As infection invaded her little body. We didn't know if she would be okay or not for several days after her emergency surgery. Then finally, on December 23rd she began to improve. Relieved is not a big enough word. She was discharged from the hospital on Christmas Day, the best gift we've ever or will ever have. We weren't "out of the woods" yet. She had an open wound that drained and she was still a very sick little girl. Weeks passed and it was such a tough time for her. Ben and I decided to get her a kitten to cheer her up. We already had adopted two older Siamese but there was room in our household for a kitten that would be Joy's alone. We looked and looked and finally found a breeder who had the cutest Siamese kittens. I was holding a little girl but Joy picked up the friskiest little boy and said she wanted that one. Of course, we went with her choice. I asked the breeder when they were born and she said, "December 23rd." Ben and I just looked at each other. No matter what is going on in our lives, what calamity may have befallen us, in places unknown to us, other things are happening. These things are the Universe's response to our needs. The Universe works like that. It has to fill voids and make balances. Unbeknownst to us, on the day that Joy began to recover, a kitten was born. Through him, as through all things, the Universe worked miracles. He became her comforter, best friend and companion for the rest of her childhood and when she left home ten years later, he stayed to fill the gap we felt by her leaving. Is he a special cat? We think so. He's really a cat, like any other. Perhaps because of the way he came to us, we are just more aware and able to see the Universe at work through him.

Anyone who has been to my house lately knows I have been very busy cleaning it out. It is very apparent when you walk in, things that have been around for years are now missing: furniture, books, knick knacks, all sorts of things. What is not so apparent, is I have also been doing this in places you cannot see, drawers, closets, attic. The last few months I have been obsessed with the need to rid myself of stuff. I look around and I think I don't need this or I don't want this, and out it goes! I'm talking about stuff I've had for many years. A friend asked me why I was doing this now. Honestly, I could not answer, except to say that it seems like it is time. I could chastise myself for holding onto things I haven't used and didn't need. I could beat myself up for being lazy or living in useless clutter but... it is that thing about time. We hold onto things until it feels right to let them go. Sometimes we aren't even aware we are holding on. Sometimes we aren't aware when we let go. But one thing I'm sure of: before the time is right, you can't get rid of anything. There's no use beating yourself up over holding on to stuff or habits or emotions or people or situations or...

We lost our kitty friend, Robin Hood on July 7, 2010. What can I say to honor his twenty years, six months and two weeks of life here on earth? The Tao Te Ching teaches that words are inadequate and it is better to be silent than to spout superfluous nonsense. Perhaps that is why it is so hard for me to express what he was and what he meant to my family. With as few words as possible, just let me say from the bestial, out of control kitten to the wise old sage and everything in between, Robin was an example of the Tao in its perfection. He had a zest for life that carried him through many illnesses and beyond, to old, old age. He never got discouraged and never gave up when there was something he knew should be his. And he knew what he wanted. He would not tolerate arguing among his people and would step in between and bellow as only he could, until the argument ceased. He unselfishly comforted the sick and bereaved. He loved to play and would be amused by the same games over and over again. He knew it was the play and not the games that was important. Most of all, he believed

that you should always strive for the highest place, because the view or perspective is better there. He did not complain when he could no longer jump to the top of the bookcases or even up on Daddy's shoulder, because the perspective was already his. Too many words. I guess there is really only one. Love.

As Robin Hood aged through the years Ben and I often thought about what we'd do after he was gone. We knew we'd have more cats. Life without cats doesn't seem to make much sense to either of us. After ten long days alone with our grief, we decided to begin the next generation of kitties. I had some doubts. I was afraid it was too soon. There are only a few souls on the earth that I love more than I loved Robin. I was afraid I wouldn't be able to love again. But everything came together and within a few hours on a Saturday afternoon Thai and Lily joined our family. On their first trip to visit our vet, Ben explained to her that it seemed soon to us but we just decided not to wait. She looked at him and said she felt if you had love to give it was wrong not to give it. I thought about that a lot. I love Robin but I can no longer give him love. What does that mean exactly? I think it meant taking care of him, honoring his life, and respecting his soul. I think love is an action verb not a noun. When a relationship ends, for whatever reason, the love stays in your heart forever. How selfish it would be to keep that love there and not share it. Every time we love, it grows stronger and every time we lose someone we love, we have more of it to give. The love I have for Robin is an immense part of my heart and always will be. Because of that, I had so much love to give to Thai and Lily. It wasn't even a question anymore. It would be wrong not to.

If we let it, the Universe will provide us with whatever we need and whatever we really want. I was pretty sure about this after we brought Thai and Lily home two years ago. When Ben and I discussed how to go about getting our new kitty friends, there were some things that were a given. I was in boy Siamese withdrawal and had to have another one. We also wanted a little girl since it had been a while without one in our lives. The boy would be another Seal Point Siamese like J.C., Pierre, Michelle, and Robin. I had a dream about the girl. I saw a little, almost completely white face with a very pink nose. I knew she would be ours. We felt we needed to contact a breeder for the boy since we specifically wanted a full-blooded Siamese, but the little girl would be a "shelter cat" like Ariel and Rosebud before her. Ben called a number from the newspaper advertising Seal Point babies for sale. We thought the boy would be hardest to find so we started with him first. For a week, he got no answer and there were no other breeders listed. Finally, on a Friday night we decided to go to the pet store where a humane society had adoptable cats. Maybe we'd have better luck there finding our girl. I could have taken them all home. There was only one who fit the description that was still in my head. She was a little older than I'd wanted. There was one other kitten that drew my attention. She was snoozing in a hammock inside her cage. She had really big ears, but what I could see of her nose wasn't pink. We came close to bringing the older cat home but at the last minute, it just didn't feel right. We came home empty handed. The next morning Ben called the breeder one last time and they answered! We drove to see the kittens. They were Siamese but not Seal Points – although their parents were. There was a Blue Point grandfather in the mix and all of the kittens but one little girl were very light. And they had long hair. It wasn't what I wanted but one little guy who was climbing the couch and bellowing at the top of his lungs caught my eye. We brought him home. He passed out in the carrier so we left him alone and went back to the pet store to get the cat we saw the night before. She was gone! But the kitten I'd seen with the ears was still there and her ears were awfully pink. They got her out and she played and played and purred and purred. We brought her home that day too. When the infection in her nose cleared up – you guessed it – there was my little pink nose. These cats were not what I wanted, not what I planned. They were perfect for us.

Two of the most important events in my life took place in the month of June. My daughter was born in June and Ben and I got married in June. So naturally, June is a big month of celebration for us. We take time out, just like most people, to honor and commemorate those days. As I was beginning to think about making plans and buying gifts, a thought occurred to me. Wouldn't it be cool if we did away with all birthdays, anniversaries, even holidays like Christmas or Mother's Day and everybody picked days at random to celebrate? At the first of every year we each could pick days to honor people and events in our lives. Heck, we wouldn't even have to limit it to just one day a year. Every Thursday after the new moon I would decide to treat my daughter as if it were her birthday! I could pick one hot day in August and mail everybody I loved a greeting card wishing them peace and goodwill and then do it again in

October if I wanted to! And just because it's Tuesday and we haven't done it for a while, Ben and I could go out and celebrate our marriage and have so much fun we'd go out again on Wednesday! That way no one would be disappointed when a date rolled around that was overlooked or not up to expectations. We'd never know when it was coming. I know, I know, it's not practical. We all have busy lives and it suits us better to have things scheduled. We don't have to think about being generous or grateful or honoring those we love except on designated days. As I said, it was just a thought.

There is no way we can live each day of our lives and avoid hurt, disappointment and loss. No matter how we live our lives and how positive we remain, sooner or later, every now and then, life hands us something we'd rather not deal with. I know all of the platitudes. We grow from adversity. What doesn't kill us makes us stronger. Maybe it is true that part of our journey here is to learn to handle hardships. Another thing I know: there is always within our grasp the means to make every hardship a little easier if we would only open ourselves to possibilities. My sister and her husband lost their beloved little dog. It was unexpected and shocking and they were devastated. The day they got the call from the vet telling them that their dog didn't make it, their son and his daughter were at the house. In the midst of all the turmoil, my sister's granddaughter was forgotten as she sat quietly at the kitchen table. Everyone was terribly upset, of course. After her son and granddaughter left my sister noticed a paper lying on the table. When she picked it up and read it, it brought a glimmer of joy to her sadness. This little first grader had calmly written a letter to the dog and to her grandmother. She was sad, too, and sorry he "was in heaven," but her main concern was that her grandmother was so sad. She drew pictures of him and a heart with her grandmother's name and offered her love as a balm to soothe some of the pain. This treasure was a work of art and found its way promptly to the front of the refrigerator. There is always a balance. For every "bad" there is a good. For every pain there is always joy. It may not erase the pain completely, and it didn't for my sister, but there is always something available if we will open our eyes. So often, these blessings go unnoticed when we are so focused on our own unhappiness. We prolong the intensity of the pain unnecessarily. A few weeks later my sister welcomed a new little boy puppy into their lives. She still misses her dog. But the balance has begun.

One of the lessons I know intellectually is that it is our attachment to people, places, things, ideas, beliefs, traditions, that causes us the most pain in our lives. Over and over again, I have congratulated myself for making progress in this area only to find out – oops, I'm not quite there yet. I have discovered a secret way to expedite this process and I would be remiss if I did not share it. All you have to do is to adopt at least two infant kittens. Immediately, everything you hold dear in your life or are attached to, becomes at-risk and you never know when something is going to be snatched from your grasp. You see, kittens live by only a very few rules but they live by them absolutely. The first rule is that everything in the world belongs to them and is their toy. The second rule is if it moves, pounce on it with all claws extended. You can ask questions later if you find it distasteful. The third rule is if it hangs in the air or is high on a shelf, it must come down, even at great bodily risk. The fourth rule is if it is on the floor, it is yours to eat no matter what it may taste like. The last rule: if mommy and daddy are asleep, it is your job to wake them up. Although most of the things we held dear and enjoyed looking at or using, are now stored safely (we hope) in the attic. I found I was attached to my cell phone charger which was chewed beyond recognition. All of our daily routines were comfortable for us too, but they've all changed. Nothing can be on the floor or in an open trash can. I'm constantly on alert. I didn't know Lily would eat toilet paper off the roll. We have to be on call at all times for explorer kitties who can fit in the most unusual places and then get stuck there. We had to design barricades all over the house and I liked my house the way it was. I was attached to my shoe laces, too – on my new tennis shoes – which now are limp and broken. I was okay when my lotus candle holder smashed to the floor. I think I miss my sleep the most. I was definitely attached to that. Ben keeps reminding me they are babies and will grow into responsible cats some day. Maybe. But in the meantime I have to keep reminding myself that all the stuff, my time, my peace and quiet, my very existence could alter at any second, including my physical body, which has endured thousands of "accidental" scratches and the one very deliberate attempt to rip off my ponytail. It's not good to be too attached to anything. It was my choice to bring new kittens into our lives and I do have to live with the consequences of the changes they bring. Besides, I find that I am becoming quite attached to Thai and Lily.

One evening as I was flipping through the stations on the TV, I came across the movie "Big." It had been years since I'd seen it, so I settled in to watch. This movie is about a boy who makes a wish to be big in front of a fortune telling machine. His wish is granted and he wakes up the next morning as an adult. Throughout the movie, we witness his trials as he attempts to put himself back to his normal age of thirteen. But something happens to him that he doesn't expect. He assumes the role of a grownup and soon begins to lose his sense of fun, adventure and innocence. It takes a dramatic encounter with his best friend to remind him that he's really a kid and reawaken his desire to return to his true self. As I watched, I realized how sad it is that we all assume the identities of grown ups, doing what we're supposed to do, letting go of our natural inclination to play, becoming suspicious and driven. Wouldn't it be cool if there were someone to remind us of who we really are?

Sometimes the lessons our kitty friends teach are so obvious and loud that I just have to give in and write them down. Recently, Thai and Lily made their first trip back to the vet in a year. It was time for their annual checkup and shots. We were a bit apprehensive about how they would handle the trip since it had been so long and we knew they wouldn't know what was going on. As we suspected, when the carriers came out and we tried to stuff them in, it was quite a battle. Eventually, they were on their way. Thai is our macho Siamese. He is a ball of energy that knows no boundaries. He is interested in everything we do and everyone who comes here and he leaps into any situation with glee and abandon. Lily, on the other hand, is gentle and shy and avoids people other than us. She is a watcher, rather than a doer, and thinks over every move before she acts. We predicted Thai would do fine, but Lily might have residual anxiety after they got home. We were wrong. As soon as their carriers were opened at the vet's and they were taken out, Thai ran to the corner of the floor under a chair and cowered. I was disappointed, because no one got to see his beautiful "Swiffer" tail. It was tucked the whole time. Lily sat up on the examining table and hissed and spit continuously until we were sure there'd be no spit left. Her best side wasn't apparent either. The exam was completed, shots were given and both cats were declared "boringly healthy." We brought them home. Lily showed no signs of stress. She resumed her usual routine, with an occasional hiss if something startled her, but Thai went to bed and slept for two days! I can only conclude that fear held in is much more exhausting than fear channeled into an expression of release. I'm not suggesting we should hiss and spit when we are afraid, but cowering in a corner is definitely an energy zapper. Perhaps we should just find a way to convey our fear in a positive way by confronting those things that make us most afraid and dealing with them. Sounds easy, but I think it is one of the hardest things there is. So, throughout the process think about our little baby girl cat and how brave she was to confront her fear and spit in its face!

Every New Year is another chance to start over, start anew, refresh, revive and generally change our lives! We celebrate the opportunity as if it were a special gift we must reach out and grasp before it escapes us! We vow this and that will be different and look forward to how much better our lives will be! Until about February, when it is apparent that nothing really has changed. We have the same feelings every time we start a new week, a new day, on our birthday – so many opportunities for failure. Every time we take a breath we are given an opportunity to change our lives. If we start slow, with something very easy, we just might succeed. Okay, you're breathing. With this out breath, decide you are not going to change anything this year. Everything stays just the same. Good. Now go though your day as you always have, breathing in and out, dreading this, longing for that, expecting this, expecting that. If you think, "I always get a cold in January," you will. If you think, "this job sucks," it will. If you think, "I hate doing this chore," you will. Let's take something simple: doing the dishes. Everybody has to do dishes at some point. Even if you have a dishwasher there is always something that has to be washed by hand. Nobody really likes dishwashing. Tonight, after dinner, fill the sink with extra bubbles. Crank up your favorite music. Play in the bubbles while you wash. Build a mountain or a funny shape. Take the soapy wooden spoon, use it as a microphone and pretend you are singing your favorite song on the radio. Use the counter as a ballet barre and do a few legs lifts on your toes. See yourself on stage as a graceful dancer. Now take a breath. You have just changed your life.

I always wanted the perfect Christmas tree. The trees in my home growing up were definitely not works of art. They were sometimes lopsided and always decorated with haste and odd ornaments that my parents could afford. One of my friends had the most beautiful tree with all the ornaments and packages color coordinated. The tips of the tree were frosted to perfection. I envied that tree. I vowed that someday I would have the perfect tree. When I was out on my own for a while and could afford to buy a new tree and new ornaments, I made an attempt at the perfect tree. For a year or two I had a tree I was pretty proud of. Then my daughter came along and brought home ornaments she made in school. What was I to do? I had to put them on the tree. Ben and I bought a little bell ornament for our first Christmas together. It didn't match my color scheme but once again, what was I to do? I had to put it on the tree every year. Then Ben inherited ornaments his grandmother had made when he was little. What was I to do? I had to put them on the tree. Friends love to give ornaments as gifts. They never matched either. What was I to do? I had to put them on the tree. Over the last few years we've lost some very special friends like Andrew and Robin and we bought ornaments to remember them and keep them close at Christmas. What was I to do? I wanted those ornaments prominently where I could see them. The first year we had Lily and Thai was the topper. With two kittens in the house, all the ornaments had to be in the top half of the tree. What was I to do? Oh well, maybe next year I'll have the perfect Christmas tree...or maybe I've had it all along.

Thai and Lily turned two in May of 2012. For their birthdays I wanted to write something for them. The problem is that I can't think of anything to write. I could tell you again how beautiful they are: about Thai's big blue slightly crossed eyes or Lily's little cotton candy pink nose. I could tell you again that Thai is a rogue who constantly loves to play and "sometimes" gets into trouble. Lily is an angel who only wants her belly rubbed and leaves her toys for me on the kitchen rug where I can find them when I return to the house. I could tell you that Thai talks all the time, and grumbles under his breath in his big boy Siamese voice and Lily squeaks when she speaks and mimics the phone when it rings. I could talk about the trials and tribulations of raising baby cats and how not prepared I was for the complete reversal of energies from our senior cats. I guess I could share the stories of sleeplessness, laughter, frustration, affection and on and on that all animal lovers experience. I must confess there were times I was not up to the challenge. They may be the cutest cats in the world but sometimes... Thai wakes me up by climbing the blinds in the bedroom. Lily stands at the top of the stairs and "sings" when I try to meditate. It is during those times and hundreds of others that I have doubted if having new kitties was such a brilliant idea. How many times do we make decisions and spend countless hours second guessing ourselves? I've done that a lot over the last two years. What if I'd just stayed catless and my home, my sleep, my sanity would all be completely intact? Then Lily touches her little pink nose to mine. Then Thai reaches out his silver/blue paw and touches my hand. Oh well. Sanity, sleep and an orderly house are somewhat overrated.

One of the teachings from the Tao Te Ching talks about the concept of yielding. Yield is my new favorite word! In our society, it is mostly associated with driving and merging onto another road or interstate highway. When we think about that, we can easily see what choices we have as we approach a yield sign. The yield sign itself is one of the few in driving that gives us a choice. We can boldly proceed into traffic without regard for other drivers. In that case, they have to yield for us or the result is an accident. We can stop and hold up other drivers behind us and wait until the road is completely clear before timidly venturing out. Or we can smoothly merge into the flow of traffic when an opening occurs. Of course, the third choice takes a bit of daring and a lot of cooperation. It also requires respect of other drivers and non-aggressive actions. To me, yield does not mean to give in or give up. It means to wait your turn and live in harmony with others around you. There are situations every day in life that require yielding. Personally, I think it is a good choice.

We get very frustrated when we feel as if we aren't able to apply what we've learned. A crisis arrives and all of it just seems to go out the window! We revert back to old ways of doing things, which usually makes things worse and we blame ourselves for not living up to what we believe. See I think it is not so easy to make changes in our lives even when we know better. I had an experience recently that demonstrated to me just how long it can take to internalize new ideas. I changed where I keep my place mats for the kitchen table. It is a little thing, I know. I just rearranged some drawers and made some room and moved the place mats. No big deal. Except I can't tell you how many times I've opened the old drawer to get those place mats out. Let's see, three meals a day times about four or five weeks – you get the picture. After about a month, I was down to maybe once a day going for the old drawer. And now, I'm happy to report, it only happens rarely, but it still happens. After fifteen plus years of getting the mats out of the same drawer it was practically impossible for me to make that change, even though I initiated the change by deciding to move where they were kept! I knew where the new location was. I picked it. Yet every meal started with the frustration of pulling open the wrong drawer. Imagine, if you can, how many habits you don't even know you have. Then think about how difficult it is to change a simple little habit like reaching for a light switch in a location from somewhere you used to live. We've all done it. Now think about changing your reactions based on new ideas. Is it any different? I don't think so. It takes time and experience to learn new reactions to the situations in our lives. We can't just will it to happen. If we could, I would not have jerked open that drawer over and over and over and over again!